CHRISTLIKE PARENTING

TAKING THE PAIN OUT OF PARENTING

D0967821

DR. GLENN I. LATHAM

GOLD LEAF PRESS

Christlike Parenting
Taking the Pain Out of Parenting

By Glenn I. Latham

Gold Leaf Press, 14675 Interurban Avenue South
Seattle, Washington 98168-4664, USA

Library of Congress Cataloging-in-Publication Data

Latham, Glenn.
Christlike parenting : taking the pain out od parenting / Glenn I. Latham
p.   cm.
ISBN 1-882723-46-5

1. Parenting- Religious aspects-Christianity. 2. Child Rearing –Religious
aspects-Christianity. I. Title
BV4529.137   1999
248.8'45-dc21   99-32778
CIP

Distributed by Brigham Distributing
435-723-6611

Cover photograph by Francois Brunelle. Used by permission
Cover design by Ron Stucki

Printed in the United States of America

10 9 8 7 6 5 4

ACKNOWLEDGMENTS

This, and related manuscripts, have been carefully and thoughtfully reviewed by many, many parents and professionals. To all of them, I feel a keen sense of gratitude.

For this work, I acknowledge in a particular way the service, support, insight, and encouragement of the following:

My wife, Louise, who has tirelessly reviewed and critiqued the manuscript. My valued colleague Dr. Paul Chance, Laurel, Delaware, for encouraging me to write this book in the first place. My long-time associate and dear Christian friend Dr. Wayne Lance, Springville, California, for his thorough reading of the text and excellent suggestions. My professional counterpart and Christian author Dr. Jim Tucker, Niles, Michigan, for his keen insights and enthusiastic endorsement of the book. Three wonderful, caring parents for their unique input: Kathy Clinton of Titusville, Florida; Elizabeth Tate of Virginia Beach, Virginia; Theresa Rottschafer of Farmington, New Mexico.

Finally, a special thanks to Jana Roberts for her tireless and tedious typing of the manuscript. God bless them all.

Author's Note

All scripture quotes are from the Authorized King James version of the Holy Bible.

CONTENTS

CHRISTLIKE PARENTING

Parents can get so bogged down with parenting woes that they are often unable to imagine that things can get any better. Too often, if they lose hope, they won't even try. A vision of Christlike parenting helps us see beyond the moment; it helps us put the highs and lows of parenting into their proper perspective. It reminds us that today is not forever. With an overarching vision of His mission, Christ Himself saw beyond His suffering into eternity and received strength to finish His work.

Even a temporary departure from Christlike parenting can bring regret. The Reverend Billy Graham, in his autobiography, *Just As I Am*, acknowledged as one of his greatest regrets the time he spent away from his children during their growing up years: "Every day I was absent from my family is gone forever" (Briggs, "Graham Looks Back," B1)

When faced with a perplexing family dilemma, I find that the best hope for resolution is found in the answer to the question, "What would Jesus do?" His path was a straight path marked by perfect love and persuasion, by gentleness and meekness, by kindness, and pure knowledge. He was full of patience and long-suffering. If everyone would parent as Christ would parent, there would be no need for the hundreds of parenting books published over the years.

The teachings of Jesus Christ, used in concert with principles of behavioral science, can benefit parents immensely as they work to solve the problems of child-rearing. Following a talk I gave that placed this science in a Christian perspective, an appreciative mother wrote to me, "I am amazed at how well it works. I have peace at last in my family. Peace at last!" On the mud wall of the

hut which Mahatma Gandhi called home hung but one adornment: a black and white picture of Jesus Christ with the inscription "He is our peace" (Fischer, 333). Regardless of your personal creed, being a Christlike parent will bring you peace.

Several reviewers of this manuscript expressed concern that the "suggestions and alternatives seem so natural and so perfect that they are almost unbelievable. The approach may seem too simple or even appear to be overly permissive for parents who have been inclined to use coercion."

Well, it is not easy, especially at first. It takes time and practice, as does learning any new skill. Whether learning to play the piano well, drive a car safely, or parent effectively, it takes time and practice. But it can be done, and the effort is worth it. Parents and teachers I work with do it all the time. The accounts of their successes would fill volumes far in excess of the number of pages in this book.

Shortly before this book went to press, a mother dropped by my office. I was leaving, she was entering, and we met at the door. She handed me a sheet of paper and said, "Here, I want you to know this." This is that letter, slightly edited to protect anonymity.

March 24, 1998
To Whom It May Concern:
One of our greatest blessings in life has been to come to know these principles. We have relied upon them as we have raised our seven children. It is amazing to me how such a few basic principles can apply to such a multiplicity of situations.

They have helped us deal with tantrums, excessive fears, fights, bed wetting, broken rules, housework, homework, and hundreds of other situations. These principles work, and they work without screaming, coercion, physical violence, or anger. Best of all, behavior is changed with the self-esteem of the child intact.

I am especially grateful for these principles and how they have impacted our lives during the past year. Our 18-year-old son has suffered from Obsessive Compulsive Disorder (OCD) for the past 11 years, but we didn't realize what it was until one year ago. We just watched as our little boy became more and more withdrawn and sad. Each year of middle school and early high school became more of a challenge to him. It wasn't until he could no longer function in school and we felt we were on the verge of losing him that we contacted Dr. Latham again. We started a journey of treatment that has proven beyond any doubt that behavioral therapy administered in a Christlike way is one of the greatest tools we have in our society today, and it has the potential of being able to help solve many of our greatest problems. After only a few months on his program, life began to make sense to our son. He was able to overcome the obsessions and compulsions that had held him captive for so long. For the first time in years, he is a happy, well-adjusted young man who has gained thirty pounds, became an Eagle Scout, is eager to go to college and is anxious to help anyone who is suffering as he did. We have seen a miracle, and although his OCD may surface throughout his life, he now has the tools to help him through it.

These Christlike principles of behavior therapy work. They are proven, they are simple, and they can help build strong, happy, functioning individuals and families. Every relationship we have can be enriched through this Christlike way of dealing with God's children. Beyond any doubt, I know that these principles are deeply anchored in eternal truths.

Though effective parenting is not necessarily easy, we typically make it a lot tougher than it should be. My wife and I were reminded of that in a stunning way during a recent weekend visit with friends of ours whom we hadn't seen in years. They have a family of seven children. Upon returning home, I made this entry in my journal:

> As we visited in their humble little home, sparsely furnished, meager and scant in every way imaginable, I thought to myself, "Indeed, in our Father's House are many mansions, and this is one of them—one of the grander ones."
>
> As parents, our friends do everything right. They pray together on bended knees. They watch TV together around the only TV set in the house—TV that is monitored and managed by the parents. They work together side-by-side. They eat together around the same table. They smile at and laugh with each other. The children play together, sharing the few toys they have. The parents tenderly hug and sweetly touch their children, and each other. They speak softly to their children. They read the scriptures together, and they help their neighbors. They worship together, and they turn their hearts and thoughts to God.
>
> In the two days we spent with them, I saw more about how to properly parent than is contained in anything I, or any other author, ever wrote on the matter. Good parenting is not rocket science.
>
> Yesterday and today I observed what was very probably the greatest lesson in effective parenting I ever witnessed, and it was delivered in a family presided over by a man I taught as a boy 36 years ago; a boy who, at the time, was classified as mildly mentally retarded.

When you think good parenting is so tough, give that some thought.

My hope is that this book will advance your progress toward becoming a Christlike parent, the only approach to parenting that can hope to be permanently right.

Glenn Latham

Chapter One

FAMILIES IN CRISIS

It's 9:30 Saturday morning. Chore time.

Mother: (To an angry 16-year-old daughter) "Honey, it's time to get our chores done."

Daughter: (Shouting in her mother's face) "Get out of my face you [!@#$%^&*]! If you think I'm going to vacuum that [!@#$%^&*] floor, you're crazy!"

Mother: (Composed and in control) "I'm sure there are other things you'd rather do, Honey, but I'm glad you understand that I expect you to vacuum the living room floor."

Daughter: (Enraged) "Are you deaf as well as dumb? Read my lips! I am NOT vacuuming that [!@#$%^&*] living room floor!"

Mother: (In complete control) "I'm sorry you're upset, but glad that you understand what your chore is." With a kindly smile, she leaves the room and goes on about her Saturday morning routine.

Daughter:	(With fire in her eyes) stands in the middle of the living room—seething.
9:35—	Mother hears the vacuum cleaner. Walking through the living room, she gently draws her fingers across her daughter's shoulders. The daughter is startled and looks up in surprise. As the mother passes, she smiles and whispers, "I love you."
9:44—	Mother is in the kitchen when the vacuuming stops.
9:46—	The daughter enters the kitchen, tears staining her checks. She puts her arms around her mother's neck, holds her tight, and in a whisper says, "Mother, I love you."

Three years later.

That 16-year-old daughter, once consumed with anger and rebellion, is now a 19-year-old college student—doing well with life and studies. Her single mother's practice of diligence, patience, long-suffering, and nonreviling are at last bringing forth fruit (3 John 1:4). This, I believe, is Christlike parenting. Free of reviling (1 Pet. 2:23). Rich in nurturing (Eph. 6:4). Completely nonreactive (Matt. 5:39).

Some might not agree with the direction I gave this overwhelmed single mother as she struggled to raise a difficult, profane, rebellious teenager. "No!" they might say. "You must never allow a child to speak with such disrespect to her mother." But I never hesitated for an instant to give that mother the direction I did. After 35 years of studying human behavior, both as a behavior analyst and a devout Christian, I am compelled to say, as did Martin Luther, "I could not have done otherwise."

Conscientious, patient, long-suffering, loving parenting—"Christlike parenting"—is my vision for parents the world over. In Proverbs we are reminded that "where there is no vision, the people perish" (29:18). We must ask ourselves, "What is our parenting vision? What is our vision for our children?" My sense is that for many parents that vision is dim. Frighteningly dim.

Historically, children have been humankind's most vulnerable—even expendable—resource. Whether it is a wicked, wroth Herod (Matt. 2:16); a genocidal Hitler or Pol Pot; a confused, pregnant teenage girl; or an out-of-control parent or baby-sitter, the result has been, and will continue to be, the same: an abused or neglected child. Our vision as a society and as individual parents, of and for our children, must improve. It must become as Christ's.

The Family in Crisis

I am not surprised that God did not rest from His labors until Adam and Eve had been joined together as "one flesh" (Gen. 2:24). Nor do I find it surprising that the first instruction given by God to this first-of-all married couples was, "Be fruitful, and multiply, and replenish the earth" (Gen. 1:28). Marriage and family are sacred things, created by God for the nurturing and good of children.

The commandment to "multiply" and be responsible parents is, beyond any doubt, the single most important responsibility ever given by God to His children. The family is, and always will be, the fundamental unit of society. The family is God's greatest masterpiece. Within it we find our greatest happiness. This is not only a fundamental religious doctrine, it is also a scientifically documented fact. Two scholars, L. Vander Post and J. Taylor, in their compelling *Testament to the Bushman*, summed it up nicely: "It remains an irrefutable social and individual premise that no culture has ever been able to provide a better shipyard for building stormproof vessels for the journey of man from the cradle to the grave than the individual nourished in a loving family" (130–31).

Today, this best of all shipyards—the loving family—is in grave danger. The mounting body of research indicates that the chance for a child to grow up in a nourishing, loving family is becoming less and less likely. It is a trend every Christian parent must resist. As stated by Mother Teresa, "If we are Christian, we must be Christlike. That is what people expect of us, that we live our Christian life to the full" (Spink, 78). And more Christlike parenting is just what our families and our children need to keep them from foundering in perilous waters.

Powerful, influential voices which convincingly advocate alternative approaches to the family are increasingly being heard. One high-profile woman characterized marriage as "silly." Another said of her relationship with her "lover": "Marriage?! I would never do a terrible thing like that to our relationship." In a recent issue of my local newspaper, I counted five articles about highly recognized entertainment, athletic, and business personalities who were unabashedly engaged in immoral relationships, conceiving and bearing children out of wedlock, and speaking of the "freedoms" they enjoyed while unencumbered by marriage. These voices are having a disturbing impact on our youth and adults. Indeed, "morals are in a global decline" ("How to Train Your Conscience," 4). As media and culture move our society toward increasingly immoral behavior, our children are put at greater and greater risk.

While such behavior bodes ill for the future of the "loving family," as Christians we must not allow the shadows of these times to fall over us. As Paul encouraged the Romans, "The night is far spent, the day is at hand: let us therefore cast off the works of darkness, and let us put on the armour of light" (Rom. 13:12).

It appears, as we study the problems of youth today, that far too many parents are failing to teach their children the difference between right and wrong; the importance of choosing what's right; and how to develop a commitment to righteous principles, values, and the sacred nature of life. Too many parents are not instilling a steady, calm influence for good and decency within the hearts of their children. How else can we can account for behavior that is becoming more violent, more wanton, and more cold-blooded; behavior for which the perpetrators are expressing little or no remorse?

As noted in the article "Why Are Kids Killing?": "Teens these days are committing crimes of incomprehensible callousness, including nearly 4000 murders a year!" (Eftimiades, et al., 46). A study of these crimes reveals that youth accused of acts of casual violence come from backgrounds that have one thing in common: they have not been taught "that the family stands for goodness, not simply comfort and intellectual achievement, but that moral excellence is honored" (Schulman, 46, 48).

Attacks on the Traditional Family

Though individual families are in crisis, the crises faced by the family as the basic unit of society are equally compelling. Although Satan considers it a victory if he destroys a family, he will have won the war if he can destroy the family institution, for that is his ultimate goal. He knows that without the family, he has won the grand prize: the hearts and souls of humankind.

For emphasis, I say it again: The family is the most basic and sacred unit of society, and God was the one who put it in place. Paul warned us that attempts would be made to alter God's plan: "Be not carried about by divers and strange doctrines" (Heb. 13:9). And there are plenty of "divers and strange doctrines" emanating from high-profile personalities and publications:

"I was so old-fashioned in that I always thought that I had to be married. But that's passé now." (Spoken by an immensely popular movie personality who was equally colossal as a failure in marriage. No wonder she would feel as she did. It's so much easier to blame the institution than it is to blame one's self.)

"Women's magazines practically recommend [adultery] as a fun and healthy activity, like buying a new shade of lipstick or vacationing in the Caribbean."

Most recently, riding the crest of the so-called sexual revolution, the cunning of the devil is seen in the form of so-called same-sex marriages. If there was ever a counterfeit attempt at creating a family, this is it. Some time ago, I was asked to prepare an affidavit stating my professional opinion on the disastrous consequences to society of same-sex marriages. They are legion. Given what we know about the God-given role of the family, it is safe to say that any union based solely on same-sex orientation is doomed to fail and destined to weaken society proportionately. It is a colossal trivialization of sex and its sacred function, a barren relationship. It is to humanity what a drought is to farming. Though it might make a few people feel good, it neither regenerates society nor improves it.

Though we must be tolerant and feel compassion for people who struggle with these weaknesses, we must not forget what the Lord expects of His children. God joined man and woman together as one flesh and commanded them to multiply and replenish the earth. That's the model. In his classic book *The Voice of the Master*, Kahlil Gibran stated it so simply, so correctly, so refreshingly: "Marriage is the union of two divinities that a third might be born on earth. It is the golden ring in a chain whose beginning is a glance, and whose ending is Eternity" (50).

Marriage is not simply a legal, civil contract. It is a sacred, divine union with an eternal purpose, "an act of covenant love" (National Council of Catholic Bishops). And "the family," noted Pope Pius XI, "is more sacred than the state, and men are begotten not for the earth and time, but for Heaven and Eternity."

In Paul's exhortation to Timothy to teach only the true doctrine of Christ, he warned that some, "having swerved [meaning missed the mark] have turned aside unto vain jangling" (1 Tim. 1:6). Well, from the standpoint of Christlike behavior, if there was ever an example of missing the mark and vain jangling, it's anything which attempts to destroy, replace, or weaken the covenant of marriage. Such attempts are what I call "spiritual lifestyle diseases" that result in self-inflicted misery and pain. They are an affront to God and an insult to His master plan for humankind. Though compassionate, I must speak plainly on this important matter.

Comfort for Grieving Parents

A few years ago, the distraught parents of an errant teenage daughter came to see me. The father, tenderly holding the hand of his grieving companion, said, "My wife is sure it's all her fault, that she is a terrible mother."

A mother sat in my office feeling crushed beneath the weight of guilt and confusion over her "failure as a mother." Tears streamed down her face as she acquainted me with her grief: "It isn't fair, Dr. Latham. It just isn't fair! I have kept myself clean and unspotted from the world so that I could be a good mother. My husband and I are honorable people. We did everything right, as we had been taught to do. I don't know what else we could have done. This just isn't fair!"

After I had delivered a talk on positive parenting to a large gathering of women, a mother sought me out for help. In desperation she lamented over the out-of-control behavior of her older children. Then, as the tears began to flow, she said, "But probably worst of all, my marriage is in serious trouble because of it. My husband and I love each other very much. We have had a wonderful marriage, but this is destroying it. Neither of us knows what to do about our children or our marriage!"

Following an address to a similar group of parents, one mother said to me, "There is so much suffering among parents. I suffer. So many of us suffer. Too many of us suffer too much." I hear that mournful lament all the time.

These are only a few examples of the anguish and confusion experienced by parents in every walk of life and in every corner of the earth who struggle with the thorns and thistles of parenthood. Several years ago while I was consulting for the Guam Department of Education, a resigned mother of a troubled teenaged son said to me, "Dr. Latham, last Sunday I took my son to church and gave him back to the Lord." Ah, if only it were that easy!

These parents are good people. They tried hard to raise their children in families which "stand for goodness." They are God-fearing people who want the best for their children and are doing the best they know how, parents who want more than anything else to be good parents. They just don't know how to do it.

Families will always be facing crises of various kinds. Families are, at times, the furnaces of affliction within which we are refined (Isa. 48:10). Modern-day parenting needs to be put into perspective. Without perspective, it is too easy to feel confused, alone, put upon, and unfairly victimized. When children stray, parents grieve. That's the way it has always been. The following four points, if remembered in times of family crisis, will help keep crises in proper perspective.

1. We are not alone.

As intense, as real and hard to bear as our grief and suffering is over the behavior of our children, we are never alone nor unique. Virtually all families suffer similarly to some degree. The history of humankind is a history of families in crisis. Following is a brief, illustrative sampling of that history:

Cain slew Abel, his brother: "Cain rose up against Abel his brother, and slew him" (Gen. 4:8). And he became "a fugitive and a vagabond in the earth" (Gen. 4:14).

Abraham grieved: "And Sarah saw the son of Hagar the Egyptian, which she had born unto Abraham, mocking.

"Wherefore she said unto Abraham, Cast out this bondwoman and her son: for the son of this bondwoman shall not be heir with my son, even with Isaac.

"And the thing was very grievous in Abraham's sight because of his son" (Gen. 21:9–11).

Isaac and his wife, Rebekah, grieved: "And Esau...took to wife Judith...the Hittite...and Bashemath...the Hittite:

"Which were a grief of mind unto Isaac and to Rebekah" (Gen. 26:34–35).

Jacob mourned and wept: "And when [Joseph's brothers] saw him afar off,...they conspired against him to slay him...

"And Reuben said unto them...cast him into this pit...

"And they took him, and cast him into a pit: and the pit was empty, there was no water in it...

"And Judah said unto his brethren, What profit is it if we slay our brother...?

"Come, and let us sell him to the Ishmaelites...

"And they drew...Joseph out of the pit, and sold Joseph to the Ishmaelites for twenty pieces of silver: and they brought Joseph into Egypt...

"And Jacob [deceived into thinking his son Joseph to be dead] rent his clothes, and put sackcloth upon his loins, and mourned for his son many days...

"And all his [deceitful] sons and all his daughters rose up to comfort him; but he refused to be comforted; and he said, For I will go down into the grave unto my son mourning. Thus his father wept for him" (Gen. 37:18–35).

The prodigal son: Went into a far country and wasted his inheritance on riotous living (Luke 15:11–13).

Mothers and fathers today mourn in pain: "We are a Christian family, devoted to our church and the principles it teaches.

Our son has left home. He can't possibly survive. What have we done wrong? How can we get our son back? We love him and we want him. How can we get him back?" (Oct. 18, 1995, personal communication).

And on and on: Samuel's sons "walked not in his ways, but turned aside after lucre, and took bribes, and perverted judgment" (1 Sam. 8:3); Jehoshaphat's son, Jehoram, "slew all his brethren with the sword" (2 Chron. 21:4).

Even this century's most influential religious personality, Billy Graham, agonized for a time over the prodigal behavior of his son (Van Biema, 147).

To her son, Harilal, Kasturbai Gandhi, the grieving wife of Mahatma Gandhi, wrote: "I do not know what to say to you. I have been pleading with you all these long years to hold yourself in check. But you have been going from bad to worse. Now you are making my very existence impossible. Think of the misery you are causing your aged parents in the evening of their lives" (Fischer, 210).

What all parents must understand and appreciate is that at times, raising a family is not easy, nor has it ever been easy. I seriously doubt that it was meant to be easy. (Though parents typically make it a whole lot more difficult than it needs to be!) Grieving, confused parents will find their best hope for comfort and direction in patterning their parenting after Christ.

2. Parenting challenges provide opportunities for parents to learn how to lead their families.

The trials and challenges of parenting provide the lessons by which we learn basic parenting skills. Mothering and fathering provide the basic parenting models for children; hence, parents must rise above the behavior of their children. Parents must be the ones who set and maintain the standard of behavior in the home. We are living in difficult times when, as never before, children are challenging the authority, roles, and positions of parents—with disastrous consequences. Isaiah saw this coming and warned us of it. "Children [will] be their princes, and babes shall rule over them...[T]he child shall behave himself proudly [meaning haughty] against the ancient,...[and] children [will be] their oppressors" (3:4, 5, 12). Sound familiar?

How often I hear resigned parents talk about having no control at home: "Our kids run our house. They run all over us!" Well, it needn't be this way, and learning to have it otherwise is, to a large extent, what this book is all about. We must learn to create and manage a safe, happy home environment within which our children have the best chance possible to develop as our Father in heaven would have them develop.

3. The traditional family unit has been created by God and tested over time.

The family unit, fashioned by God Himself, is the only family unit acceptable to God. Any and all others are bogus; they are counterfeit! To affiliate ourselves with any other is to cheat our souls and allow ourselves to be deceived, to be "carried about with divers and strange doctrines" (Heb. 13:9). The family unit is the enduring unit. Over time, it has proven its durability. The eminent sociologist Margaret Mead, speaking of the many alternatives to the family "invented" by humankind, noted that "the family always creeps back."

4. The Lord stands ready to help all parents.

Most important, the best source of comfort in times of crisis is the Lord: "Seek ye first the kingdom of God, and his righteousness" (Matt. 6: 33).

The master model of moral excellence is Jesus Christ. His is the only sure and enduring model. His teachings and His example were given to show us how to love and lead our children. When things go wrong, only He can heal our hearts, and our families.

No one holds parents to a higher standard of performance than does the Lord. The essence of His teachings allows no other conclusions. To Timothy, Paul wrote, "For if a man know not now to rule his own house, how shall he take care of the Church of God?" (1 Tim. 3:5). Of a child brought to Him to be healed, Christ proclaimed, "Whosoever shall receive this child in my name receiveth me" (Luke 9:48). And to his disciples, Christ said of children, "of such is the kingdom of heaven" (Matt. 19:14). Richard M. Milnes, a nineteenth-century English poet, wrote, "The Christian home is the Master's workshop where the processes of character molding are silently, lovingly, and faithfully carried out" (Bradley, 553). And just for emphasis: "Take heed that ye despise not one of these little ones.... [It] is not the will of your Father which is in heaven, that one of these little ones should perish" (Matt. 18:10, 14). This is strong doctrine and a heavy responsibility, but true nonetheless.

To whom does it not apply? Parents who are corporate executives or busy political/civic leaders? Young parents struggling to continue their education? Couples hardly able to make ends meet? Single parents frantically, sometimes desperately, working alone to keep the family together and solvent? Older parents helping their children and grandchildren? I sense from reading the scriptures that no one is exempt. It is better that our house is in order than our business, our profession, our studies, or any of our other areas of responsibility.

As difficult and challenging as life can sometimes be, no challenge carries with it more meaning, nor demands more attention from parents, than that of nurturing and teaching their children. Can any Christian parent seriously question the Lord's position on that matter? Think about it.

The Christlike Parent

What, then, is the measure of a Christian parent, and what can be expected of Christian parenting? As I read the scriptures, study the teachings of Christ, and consider what research in human behavior has taught us, I have concluded that within the Christian perspective, the measure of a "good parent" is eightfold:

1. Good parents teach their children to behave as Christ would behave, which includes the broad Christian message of honesty, decency, kindness, love of God and fellowman, and so on.

2. Good parents are living examples to their children of the principles and teachings of Christ.

3. Good parents create within their homes a safe, positive, happy, noncoercive, nonabusive environment where

consequences are consistently and lovingly applied; an environment where children behave well in order to enjoy the positive benefits of behaving well, rather than to avoid the negative consequences of behaving badly.

4. Good parents allow their children to exercise their moral agency, then calmly and patiently let consequences do the teaching.

5. Good parents never give up; they pray for their children continually, with faith in Christ.

6. Good parents are continually learning and applying better, more effective parenting skills.

7. Good parents rise above the misbehavior of their children and happily and confidently get on with life and continue in the faith together.

8. Good parents put parenting above all other earthly endeavors.

Collectively, this is what I have chosen to call the Christlike parent. When these conditions are met, good parenting has been achieved. This is not to say that to be a good parent one never makes mistakes or that nothing will ever go wrong. To draw such a conclusion is shallow, needlessly self-deprecating, and potentially self-destructive: "Regrets and disappointments rise up like ghosts from the past. A sense of failure can lead you into a valley of shame which, in turn, can isolate you from your children, your family, and other community support" (National Council of Catholic Bishops, 1997).

Well-meaning parents who have tried their best should avoid the temptation of using their children's behavior as the measure of their success as parents. If children's behavior were the sole measure of good parenting, our heavenly Father would not qualify. Through Isaiah, the Lord lamented, "I have nourished and brought up children, and they have rebelled against me" (Isa. 1:2). Remember this: Even with the best of parenting, there is always the risk that some children will stray.

A contemporary religious leader has noted that "it is a great challenge to raise a family in the darkening mists of our moral environment. The measure of our success as parents...will not rest solely on how our children turn out. That judgment would be just only if we could raise our families in a perfectly moral environment, and that now is not possible.

"It is not uncommon for responsible parents to lose one of their children, for a time, to influences over which they have no control. They agonize over rebellious sons or daughters. They are puzzled over why they are so helpless when they have tried so hard to do what they should" (Packer, "Our Moral Environment," 68).

On a similar note,

> we should never let Satan fool us into thinking that all is lost. Let us take pride in the good and right things we have done; reject and cast out of our lives those things that are wrong; look to the Lord for forgiveness, strength, and comfort; and then move onward.
>
> A successful parent is one who has loved, one who has sacrificed, and one who has cared for, taught, and ministered to the needs of a child. If you have done all of these and your child is still wayward or troublesome or worldly, it could well be that you are, nevertheless, a successful parent.
>
> My concern...is that there are parents who may be pronouncing harsh judgments upon themselves and may be allowing these feelings to destroy their lives, when in fact they have done their best and should continue in faith. (Hunter, "Parents' Concern for Children," 65)

Parenting is a risky enterprise, the risks of which can be avoided only by not being a parent. I am reminded of the parents who, disillusioned with family life and fed up with the "crying and the fighting, and the asking for new toys," gave their three children up for adoption! "It was getting to be very discouraging," they whined. "We're both still young, and we have lots of other interests. After four years of parenting, we are ready to move on." So they gave their children away!

I have concluded that parenting is a refining process. In revealing His purposes to Israel, the Lord said, "I have refined thee...; I have chosen thee in the furnace of affliction" (Isa. 48:10). I consider this to be a fitting analogy to the refining of parents. I speak with some experience when I say that at times the home can become a furnace of affliction. As the parents of six children and the grandparents/great grandparents of twenty-two (and counting), Louise and I know something of the heights and depths of parenting. Having been refined by it, my sweetheart and I are better because of it. We would do it again without hesitation.

As I have occasionally noted in some of my talks, my wife and I are happy to be the parents of six children—who are all raised! But now we are grandparents, so it's not over for us yet, thankfully. If we love grandparenting as much as we love parenting, the joy that awaits us is unimaginable. With the passage of time, the challenges grow and the blessings increase.

To all who have children, regardless of how those children behave, I say be happy and count your blessings. To those contemplating parenthood, I say be happy and soon you'll be counting blessings available to you through no other means.

In either case, my appeal to all parents, new or seasoned, is to parent as Christ would parent. "Please remember this one thing. If our lives...are centered upon Jesus Christ...nothing can ever go *permanently* wrong. On the other hand, if our lives are not centered on the Savior and his teachings, no other success can ever be *permanently* right" (Hunter, "Following the Master," 21; emphasis added).

Families are in crisis—always have been and always will be. That's how Satan wants it; that's his way. But there is an antidote, a tonic, a salve. It's called Christ's way.

I leave you here with Paul's caution and appeal to the Ephesians: "Let no man deceive you with vain words." "Walk in love, as Christ also hath loved us" (5:6 and 2).

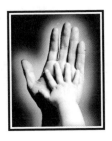

Chapter Two

"Be of Good Cheer"

Troubled, and likely fearing for their lives as they were "tossed with waves" in a sea of "contrary" winds (Matt. 14:24), Jesus' disciples were comforted and assured when their Master said, "Be of good cheer; it is I; be not afraid" (Matt.4:27). What great advice to anguishing parents tossed about by the contrary winds of our tumultuous and troubled environment. Look to Christ, be as Christ; be not afraid, be of good cheer.

When children misbehave, go astray, deny the teachings of their parents, seek their own counsels in darkness, turn their backs on the commandments of God, and invite turmoil into their lives and the lives of their families, it is no wonder parents despair, suffer much grief, and even become ill. In studying the behavior of grieving parents, I have observed a number of common physical responses provoked by wayward children. The following is a description typical of grieving parents:

1. Frowns, scowls, and looks of despair invade their faces.
2. Their head and shoulders droop.

3. They seldom smile or laugh, and their countenance falls.

4. They lose the spring in their step and tend to shuffle along.

5. The lilt in their voice is replaced by a monotone.

6. There is little physical or verbal animation. Rather than gesturing expressively, their hands remain limp at their sides or in their laps; rather than punctuating their speech with colorful anecdotes and creative turns of phrase, they say as little as possible while using dull, unimaginative language.

7. They tend to fear the worst, often hardly being able to imagine things ever being better. Affection for the child is tempered with a sense of resignation: "He is basically a good boy and we love him, but..."

None of this is attractive to the wayward child. None of this is helpful to the wayward child. It is no wonder to me that repeatedly, in times of despair and crisis, the Savior told the distressed, "Be of good cheer."

Values Versus Compliance

As I have studied and treated parenting problems of the past generation, I have noticed a disturbing shift in parental concerns from values to compliance. When I was a boy, I don't recall my mother ever saying to me "Do this. Do that. Don't do this. Don't do that." Rather, I clearly recall her encouraging me to be honest, kind, hardworking, helpful, fair, tolerant, and so on. We refer to these as "common moral decencies because they maximize human happiness and minimize suffering" (Newman, et al., 279). They are the moorings of any stable society, but they are becoming less and less evident and weaker by the day. On the golf course, whenever I let a faster playing group play through, they rarely say thank you, especially young people. Road rage is killing people every year. Cheating on exams is just the thing to do. I sometimes get the feeling that what we need is another Great Depression, or a similar trauma, to bring us together and to our knees.

A key facet of Christlike parenting is for parents to move toward teaching values and being less concerned about compliance and conformity. Remember, "Socrates, Jesus Christ, Gandhi, and Martin Luther King were not conformists. The Nazis were" (Bear, 365), as are all totalitarians. Forced conformance and compliance creates a coercive environment, which in turn encourages children to escape, avoid, and countercoerce (meaning get even) (Sidman, p. 109). It is a natural law of human behavior. You can count on it.

Teaching children common moral values and decency requires that we consciously create an environment within which children have opportunities to serve and help others, practice empathy and understanding, practice basic social graces (e.g., using "please," "thank you," "you're welcome," "excuse me"), put the needs of others ahead of theirs, exercise restraint and self-control, work hard, and so on. These must be learned, and they are learned best in a well-designed learning environment where they are utilized and practiced. Create such an environment, and you will soon create good cheer. I suggest the following for your consideration:

1. Make a list of the basic moral values you want your children to learn and practice.
Write them down:
—kindness
—honesty
—civility
—and so on
Have the list posted where you see it often as a reminder of what you are looking for, and when you see your children behaving in a way consistent with those values, acknowledge that behavior:

Setting: One child is kind to others.
Parent: "Thank you for being kind. That was wonderful."

Setting: Children at the dinner table are saying "please" and "thank you."
Parent: "Words like that are music to my ears. You're so appreciative. Thanks tons."

Setting: You've just had an enjoyable conversation and visit with a child.

Parent: "I really enjoyed that visit. You're so pleasant to be with."

Setting: You're playing a game and a child calls an error on himself, resulting in the loss of a turn or earned points.

Parent: "That was such a lovely, honest thing to do. It makes having you around and playing games with you such fun."

Setting: A son or daughter comes home tired, sweaty, and even dirty from helping someone in distress, like pushing a stalled car.

Parent: "Thank you for helping. That was a kind and generous thing to do."

The key to this suggestion is that parents know in advance what behaviors to look for, then acknowledge them when they appear. If these reminders are not prominently displayed, it's "out of sight, out of mind," and a host of wonderful things happen without being acknowledged.

2. Don't be blinded by the "noise."

Recently I came upon a driver whose car had stalled. As I got out of my car to help, a number of "upstanding" citizens just whizzed by. Then an old clunker stopped and out jumped a couple of boys with long hair, earrings, beads, baggy trousers—the whole nine yards. "Can we help?" they asked cheerfully, and in a flash the stalled car was safely out of harm's way.

The long hair, earrings, beads, baggy trousers were all what we call "behavioral noise." When you set out to acknowledge acts of decency and goodness, be sure to not let the "noise" blind you.

When sincere expressions of appreciation were extended to these boys, they were genuinely pleased, and an opportunity was seized to reward decency, regardless of how it was dressed and groomed. It is predictable that in the future these boys will respond in a similar way to others in need.

3. Embellish your verbal praise by going beyond compliance to values.

For example:

Setting: A child completes an assigned task.

Parent: (Acknowledging compliance) "Thanks for getting your chore done."

(Going beyond compliance to values) "You're a dependable girl. That's wonderful."

Setting: A child returns home from the store where he or she has done some grocery shopping for the family. The change returned to the parent was correct to the penny.

Parent: (Acknowledging compliance) "Thanks, Honey, for returning the change."

(Going beyond compliance to values) "Your commitment to honesty as well as being helpful are super. Thanks tons."

Do you get the picture? Doing what was told/asked/assigned (that is, complying) was acknowledged, and that's good. But with the momentum of that positive behavior being nudged along by piggybacking onto it a value statement, the child comes to see himself or herself as not only a doer of good things, but as a *good person* who does good things.

When we teach our children values, their lives are richer for it, as are the lives of others. Louise and I worked hard during our child-rearing years to teach our children to be decent people, and they are decent people: generous, kind, helpful, honest, compassionate. Every one of them. I suspect this is the kind of thing Paul had in mind in his epistle to Titus when he wrote of "behaviour as becometh holiness" (Titus 2:3), a significant leap beyond mere compliant behavior.

4. Endear humankind's real heroes to your children.

Among mine are Mother Teresa, Billy Graham, Desmond Tutu, Gordon B. Hinckley, and the neighbor who makes it an important part of life to serve others, with no thought of anything in return. These are cheerful givers, and "God loveth a cheerful giver" (2 Cor. 9:7).

We who address the behavioral ills of these convoluted times are troubled by the personalities our children are taking as role models. I needn't take time here to belabor that point. You know what I mean. So what should be done about it? Simple! Just talk to your children about real heroes. Learn something about them, then share that with your children.

Here's a suggestion for starters. At supper, tell your children of a dream Mother Teresa had: "I went to St. Peter, but he would not let me in, saying: 'There are no slums in heaven.'" (A Gift for God: Prayers and Meditation, 7). Then ask, "Why would St. Peter want to send Mother Teresa back to earth to the slums? She's such a wonderful person. If anyone deserves to go to heaven, she does. Why would St. Peter rather have her in the slums than in heaven?" Then watch a real hero come alive in your children's lives as they answer the question.

Considerable research has been done to determine what it is that people really value in others. One study, quite reflective of such studies generally, reported that "greatness" in the popular sense was not what was most admired. Rather, those held in "highest esteem" were "those who mastered a hard lot with their heads held high" (Frankl, 149).

Introduce your children to people who have mastered a "hard lot with their heads held high," to those who cheerfully serve others and ask nothing in return. Remind them of the many people Christ helped, and He never sent a bill to one of them! Now there's a real hero to begin with! Remind them also that Christ held His head high. He faced adversity with dignity, so much so that Pilate "marvelled greatly" (Matt. 27:14). On the eve of the darkest moment in Christ's life on earth, He said to his apostles, "In the world ye shall have tribulation: but be of good cheer" (John 16:33). Heroes don't get any better than that!

Why do I talk of values and heroes in a chapter on cheer? Because people with values and of heroic proportions are people of good cheer. Like Christ, they have adversity, but they remain cheerful.

One of my very favorite scriptures is found in 2 Corinthians, the fourth chapter. Consider carefully these words of Paul to the Corinthians:

> We are troubled on every side, yet not distressed; we are perplexed, but not in despair;
> Persecuted, but not forsaken; cast down, but not destroyed;
> ...that the life also of Jesus might be made manifest in our body.
> For our light afflictions, which but for a moment, worketh for us a far more exceeding and eternal weight of glory." (8–10, 17)

Is that great, or what?

I believe that is the message of Christ to despairing parents: be of good cheer and let optimism rise above afflictions. That is how Christ would parent. Parents tend to be too prone to guilt and too quick to assume that all is lost, too convinced that today is forever, that only one hundred percent goodness one hundred percent of the time will do.

Parental Guilt

I have been impressed that parents seldom miss an opportunity to feel guilty about their perceived shortcomings as parents. By keeping a keen eye open for reasons to feel guilty, they almost never come up disappointed. It is as though they have a need to suffer guilt and shame for their children's wrongdoings. Such self-imposed burdens and undeserved guilt are absolutely purposeless. They not only do no good, but they can do considerable harm by encouraging in parents unreasonable feelings of failure and inadequacy that further impair their effectiveness while convincing children that they are indeed bad children. Neither circumstance is purposeful or constructive.

The fact is that even the most straight-arrow children will sometimes make poor decisions which put their lives at odds with what is in their best interest and the teachings of Christ. For some parents, getting good grades, being a student leader, going to college, being a responsible citizen, and so on, though laudable, are not sufficient. Complete parental acceptance and satisfaction are realized only when these accomplishments are accompanied by behaviors that characterize children as "spiritually" responsible. This typically means going to church, being "clean cut," and so on.

As important as these are in shaping a child's spiritual character, the violation of any or all of them by children who have been taught otherwise and raised in a Christian environment is not sufficient justification for parents to feel guilty, responsible, or inadequate. In fact, such feelings, with their outpourings of agony, often communicate to children that their behavior is beyond hope. They are given the impression that if they are not one hundred percent socially and religiously responsible, they have missed the mark entirely; they are "unclean." Such a perception of self can and often does drive children even further from family ties, religious affiliation and participation, and frequently from being socially responsible, decent people as well.

Surely, our greatest parental hope is that our children attain a state of righteousness. It is the only sure road to happiness. But to attain such a state requires that they be decent as well as compliant. I know many, many young people who are not "righteous" in the usual sense. But they are wonderfully decent people with many praiseworthy qualities. They are not "devout" in the sense that they attend church faithfully, dress or groom themselves traditionally, or publicly declare their devotions, but they are kind, honest, hard working, concerned for others, and unselfish. Unfortunately, many of their parents tend to discount and even trivialize that decency because the child doesn't participate fully in their church.

Conversely, I know young people who attend all of their church meetings, but whose daily behavior is woefully lacking when it comes to matters of decency. They use profanity without hesitation; they bad mouth others; they cheat on their exams at school; and they are morally loose and coarse. But their parents are content because they are "clean cut" and at church every Sunday.

In the process of encouraging and recognizing righteousness, we must not forget decency. Mr. Dave Thomas, founder of Wendy's restaurants, speaks passionately about the need for "honesty, integrity, and hard work within the laws of God and man," accompanied by a "burning desire to be nice" (Thomas, "Doing the Right Thing"). As parents, we must recognize and acknowledge these behaviors in our children whether they are active church goers or not, for decency is an important part of "righteousness."

What every parent must realize is that today is not forever. Children move in and out of church activity and commitment to Christian principles. Their levels of devotion and commitment ebb and flow. The key to surviving these undulations is to love our children no matter how they behave. That's Christ's message (Luke 15:1–7).

Parents are often so quick to feel guilty because of the behavior of their children. They confuse guilt with disappointment and sins with mistakes. As parents, we must make a distinction between sins and mistakes. Guilt is a by-product of sin; disappointment is a by-product of a mistake. Sin is committed when we consciously and knowingly choose evil over good. The consequence of that is guilt. And that's good. Guilt is to the soul what pain is to the body; it reminds us that something is the matter and needs to change. If we ignore pain or guilt, we stand to suffer even more.

Disappointment, on the other hand, is a by-product of a mistake, a poor choice between what one hopes is good, better, or best. In either instance, whether it is disappointment generated by mistakes or guilt generated by sins, something must change before there is any hope that things will get better. Wallowing in guilt is not an adequate response, nor is languishing in a thorny bed of poor choices.

A young woman came to me almost distraught with guilt over her circumstances. She was involved in an immoral relationship with a man and had every reason to feel guilty. After discussing her problem, I made some very precise and direct suggestions as to how she could put her life in order. First among those, of course, was that she immediately and permanently terminate her immoral behavior. Her response nearly blew me away. She said, "Oh, I can't do that. I enjoy it too much. I just don't want to feel guilty about it."

As absurd as that is, I am continually amazed at the number of parents I work with who are overcome with guilt and regret about their "failure" as parents, but who refuse to do what needs to be done to find relief through improved parenting. It is as though they believe that with a sufficient amount of disappointment or guilt, they will be absolved of further responsibility and excused from needing to change.

Rather than being tormented by guilt and disappointment we should change whatever it is that produces them. It is really as simple as that. We can't continue to do what we have been doing and expect different results. Whether the behavior was produced by sin or mistakes is not the issue—nor are feelings of guilt or disappointment. The issue is one of changing parental conduct for the better.

Some people have great difficulty with this. "What about the kid's responsibility?" they say. "He gets off scot free. Why do I have to do all the changing?!" I call this a "hardened" response. We observe it often in people who try to lessen the gravity of their sins or mistakes by using self-serving rationalizations: "I'm not the only hypocrite you know. Christianity is full of them." They conveniently assume a more permissive value system: "I just don't believe that naive, goody-goody stuff anymore. I've progressed to a higher mentality." They take a defeatist position: "So what! It's my life. Just get off my back." They are soon hardened toward the very warnings designed to alert them to the dangers of their behavior. If we appropriately act upon earned feelings of guilt and disappointment, whether as parents or individuals, they can save us a lot of grief and remorse. But we must act!

Three Lessons

In our actions, there are three important lessons for all parents:

1. More than anything else, always love your children.

Louise and I love parenting because we love our children. We haven't always been pleased with the things our children have done or the choices they have made, but we have always loved them. To keep our love for them above all else, the focus of our affection is on *them*, not on their foibles. Our children have achieved considerable success in life, for which we are happy. But that is not why we love them. We love them not because of what they have accomplished materially or socially, but because of who they are: our heaven-sent children. Don't ever forget, Mom and Dad, that your children came to you from heaven, as gifts of God. Think about it! When you look at your children, think of them as the objects of your love, not the objects of your pride or displeasure.

Babies, infants, and little children are easy to love. They seem to appreciate their parents' love. They want to be near their parents. They raise their hands and lovingly appeal: "Hold me." They spontaneously hug and kiss their parents. Their innocence makes them so attractive and desirable. Ask a child, "Do you love your Mommy/Daddy," and almost without hesitation or exception they answer, "Yes."

Loving adolescent children is sometimes more difficult. They tend to see their parents as resources rather than objects of love and affection. They are often embarrassed to even be seen with their parents. Parents are weird. Ask teenagers, "Do you love your parents," and they will typically answer, "Well, yes, but..." The beginnings of qualified love emerge day-by-day. Teenagers look less and less like heaven-sent gifts and more and more like life's greatest challenges.

Ask parents if they love their little ones, and they will quickly answer, "Yes." Ask parents if they love their teenagers, and they will typically answer, "Yes, but..." or "Yes, because..." There seems to exist a need to explain one's love. Yet we must love our children. That is our first responsibility. We would never question God's unqualified love for all of His children, regardless of how old they are or how they behave. We needn't wonder, therefore, how our heavenly Father expects us to feel about our children no matter how old they are, or how they behave.

2. Maintain a Christlike countenance.

The sights, sounds, and thoughts of our children can "trigger" responses that say a lot about how we feel about them and about being a parent. Dr. Philip Teitelbaum, an eminent behavioral physiologist at the University of Florida, found in his study of the "range of allied reflexes" that an entire range (sequence) of behaviors can be set into motion by a single "trigger" behavior. Though his work has been with people suffering from Parkinson's disease, it has relevance to parents suffering over the behavior of their children.

Generalizing from Dr. Teitelbaum's work, I advise parents to be prepared with a pleasant, loving thought about their children, a thought that can "trigger" a range of allied thoughts of love and affection, no matter how their children are behaving. The admonition of Christ to His disciples to be of good cheer is so relevant in this regard.

I have observed that when parents despairingly look at, think about, or talk about a disobedient, annoying, wayward child, that becomes the "trigger" that sets into motion a range of responses (behaviors) including frowning, a drooping of the head and shoulders, a falling of the parent's countenance, a lethargic gait, a resigned shaking of the head, and so on. It is predictable, it is defeating, and if the child is present, it communicates the terrible message that the child is not the only one whose behavior is out of control.

The skill parents must learn is to smile, not frown. Parents must learn to think love for the child, to avoid anxiety or needless worry about the child, to direct attention *away* from the negative and *toward* the positive. These are all trigger behaviors that will facilitate and set into motion a healthy, optimistic range of allied responses: head and shoulders held high, smiles and laughter, a lilting voice, and an animated demeanor. These communicate a powerful and positive message to children and give them confidence that despite their own low-level-of-maturity behavior, Mom and Dad have it together. Kids love it when moms and dads have it together!

Some years ago while I was giving a talk to a large gathering of parents, a mother raised her hand and asked, "What am I to do with my seventeen-year-old son? I can't think of anything good about him to acknowledge. He looks bad, he smells bad, he is bad. I haven't even seen him for several days. What am I supposed to do when he comes home?" I asked what she usually did, and she said, "I tell him he's a stinking mess and needs to shape up."

I asked her what his typical response was. She said, "Oh, he just grunts at me and goes to his room, then I don't see him again for several days."

I asked her if she would try a different response; a positive one, by looking for something good to acknowledge. I suggested, then, "When he comes home, lift your head high, square your shoulders, smile, look him right in the eye, and say, 'Good breathing, Son.'" She looked at me like I was kidding and asked, "What did you say?"

I repeated what I had told her and added, "Let him know you're glad he's home safe and sound, that you've been concerned about him." I also assured her that I was dead serious about what I had advised her to do.

A few days later, I got a phone call. It was that mother. She excitedly told me what had happened. It went something like this: "My son came home last night. He looked bad, he smelled bad, and I'm sure he had been bad. Fighting off the urge to be negative, I stood tall, smiled, looked him right in the eye, and said, 'Good breathing, Son.' He looked at me as though he hadn't understood what I said and asked, 'What did you say, Mother?' I answered, 'I'm glad you're home safe and sound and still breathing, Son. I've been worried about you!'

"We just stood there looking at each other. Then he smiled back, walked over to me, put his arms around me, kissed my cheek, and told me he loved me." At last, mother was safe.

Be careful of the range of allied behaviors triggered by your children. "Lift up your head and be of good cheer." Your children will love it, and you will love them. You will make yourself safe to come home to.

Parents need to understand something important about countenance and behavior. When one's countenance falls, the door is open to invite inappropriate behavior. That is another natural law of human behavior. When one's countenance is up—bright and cheery—the incidence and magnitude of inappropriate behavior decrease. Conversely, when one's countenance is low—dark and gloomy—the incidence and magnitude of inappropriate behavior increase. As you read news accounts of people doing shameful and outrageous things, you will read occasionally that shortly before they behaved so badly, something significant happened to lower the general level of positive reinforcement in their lives. The assassination of Yitzhak Rabin, prime minister of Israel, is a classic example. The news reported that his assassin, shortly before he committed his heinous crime, had broken up with his girlfriend, was "down," and wanted attention.

The greatest, most illustrative example of the relationship between a fallen countenance and awful behavior is found in Genesis. It's the account of Cain's murder of his brother Abel. Cain didn't wake up one morning after a good night's sleep, step outside into the fresh morning air, stretch deliciously, then exclaim, "What a great day! The sky is blue, the sun is shining. I think I'll kill Abel today." No. The scriptures tell us that "Cain was very wroth, and his countenance fell...[and he] rose up against Abel his brother, and slew him" (Gen. 4:5, 8).

When we let things get to us, when we stew in our misery rather than redirect our behavior into healthy paths, we become wroth, our countenance falls, and we do and say mean and ugly things, often to those we love. And like feathers in the wind those things can never be gathered up. We become a hiss and a byword to our children. A mark is put upon us: abuser, offender, etc. That is not Christ's way. And no amount of rationalizing will make it Christ's way!

Norman Vincent Peale gave us good, doable advice: "Keep your emotions in balance, keep them level; keep your sense of humor.... Ease up.... Don't take things so seriously, yourself included.... Forget it, and look to the future. There is healing for you in the future. Trust God. God loves you" (Peale, 5).

Do you get the message here? Keep a Christlike countenance. Put a smile on your face. It can be done. In Viktor Frankl's gripping account of his dreadful years in Nazi concentration camps, he wrote of the preserving power of a cheerful countenance which could afford one "an ability to rise above any situation, even if only for a few seconds" (54). And sometimes that's all it takes. A few seconds of cheer can have a *stunning* effect on the momentum of a behavior. It can stop negative behavior dead in its tracks, while redirecting behavior and creating an "arena of comfort."

In their delightful book *Glimpses of God's Love*, James and Priscilla Tucker make this absolutely vital point: "With all that we as Christians have to be thankful for, we should never stop smiling in our hearts. And those heart smiles will often erupt onto our faces, giving us a special radiance resulting from feeling the joy of Jesus deep in our heart" (279).

3. Avoid agonizing over "What did I do wrong?"

This is a form of introspection [looking inward] that is virtually always doomed to make a person feel worse. In my years working with parents in distress, I've heard the lament "What did I do wrong?" a thousand times, I'm sure. But I've yet to have a parent tell me, "You know, I asked myself what I had done wrong, looked inwardly into the deep, dark recesses of my past, found what I did wrong, fixed it, and now everything is okay." Never!

When we introspect like this, things typically get worse for at least a couple of reasons. First, while looking for mistakes, we tend to beat up on ourselves. Since we are looking only for things we did wrong, we can easily find something faulty: "You idiot! How could you have done such a stupid thing? There is no hope for you. You have no clue about how to be a decent parent. The kids would be better off if I just walked out of their lives. No wonder they hate me. All I do is scream at them for every little thing. I'd hate me too. In fact, I do hate me!" What has such thinking accomplished? For starters, it has reinforced in the parent's mind feelings of doubt, inadequacy, stupidity, and self-hate. That's what the parent went looking for, and that's what the parent found. It's a self-fulfilling prophecy.

Secondly, there are no answers to be found that way. Dr. Jefferson Fish of St. John's University, in his article "Does Problem Behavior Just Happen?" noted: "Attempts to achieve insight [by focusing on the origins of a behavior] make changes more difficult" (7). Remember that: Self-probing does not produce solutions, it only makes finding a solution more difficult! "Problem talk," writes Dr. Fish, "leads to negative thoughts [that lead to the expectation of] negative outcomes. *Knowledge of the problem behavior is unnecessary to change.* [Rather] 'solution talk' encourages positive thoughts and expectancies" (6; emphasis added). This includes asking one's self questions like "What do you want?" and "What can you do differently?" (7). The focus here is on the future, not the past.

The message to parents is clear: We must quit beating up on ourselves through a lot of useless introspection and mucking around in the past and get on with life. We must change what needs to be changed.

Solution Thinking

Learning new skills takes study and practice. Rather than looking for problems, parents need to become "solution thinkers." An effective strategy parents can learn and use to make the change from problem thinking to solution thinking is called covert conditioning, which issues from the work of my good friend Dr. Joseph Cautela, of Cambridge, Massachusetts. In this instance, "covert" refers to behaviors that are not obvious, such as thoughts and feelings. "Conditioning" means to modify or shape in a certain way. "Covert conditioning," therefore, means to modify or shape our thoughts by imagining the way we should behave (called the target behavior), then immediately following this with happy, pleasant thoughts about ourselves (10).

Simply put, it is changing the way we think by making solution thinking more pleasant and reinforcing than problem thinking. In other words, act the way you want to be and soon you'll be the way you act. It is a "psychology of wellness" (Rhodes, 9), a state of being that has been linked to lower rates of suicide and depression, an increase of marital and overall life satisfaction, an increased ability to cope, and, in children, the development of resiliency.

Suppose I have been thinking unpleasant, self-denigrating thoughts about myself as a parent. For example, "If you had a brain in your head, you'd be a decent father." To reshape or recondition that negative thinking, in addition to being a decent father, I would replace negative thoughts with healthier thoughts. I would say to myself, "Though parenting isn't always easy, I am trying hard to do better each day. For example, today I told each of my children I love them. I hope it made them feel as good as it made me feel." After thinking that thought, I would then say to myself, "That's much better. You are doing well." This is a form of covert conditioning, and it can do wonders in triggering a healthy, positive range of healthy responses.

Even though problem thinking is rarely if ever good for us, it can nevertheless be very self-reinforcing, and (now think about this carefully) anything that immediately reinforces a behavior has the powerful effect of keeping that behavior going. Problem thinking breeds problem thinking. Problem thinking is a self-reinforcing covert behavior. It is remarkable how often we pet our pet problems!

People do all kinds of unhealthy things they know are not good for them. Often they are displeased with themselves when they do them and wish they would stop. After they have done them and been self-reinforced for doing so, they frequently make vows never to behave that way again. But, alas, they do! And why? Because behaving that way is more reinforcing at the moment than is behaving some other way. Vowing to behave better, not wanting to behave badly, knowing they shouldn't behave as they are, having a good attitude about doing better things, desiring to change, and so on are absolutely meaningless as long as the reinforcing effects of continuing to do something unhealthy are more powerful than the reinforcing effects of doing something better. Saying to ourselves, "I am not going to do that again," is a waste of breath unless we immediately do something different *that is more reinforcing.*

It is interesting to me that Christ concluded his Sermon on the Mount with a statement about doing rather than merely saying:

> Not every one that *saith* unto me, Lord, Lord, shall enter into the kingdom of heaven; but he that *doeth the will of my Father* which is in heaven. (Matt. 7:21; emphasis added)

Doing is the key. But being reinforced for doing is what keeps the doing going. Now, let's apply the strategy of covert conditioning to making the switch from problem thinking to solution thinking using what are called "incompatible behaviors."

Whenever a problem thought comes into your head: "I blew it again! How could I have been so stupid?" switch immediately to a healthy incompatible thought (this is called the "target behavior"). An incompatible thought is a covert behavior that competes with the problem thought; that is, if you think of the healthy incompatible thought longer than the unhealthy problem thought, the healthy thought wins.

Here's how I do it, and it works very well. When an unhealthy problem thought comes into my head, I immediately switch my thinking to a healthy incompatible behavior: I begin reciting, in order, the books of the Old Testament. If the competition between the unhealthy thought and the healthy thought is fierce, and the healthy thought has not won by the time I say "Malachi," I continue by reciting the books of the New Testament. Rarely does the unhealthy thought survive long enough to make it to Revelation. But if it does, I have other incompatible behaviors ready to call to my defense.

To completely clear the playing field of any stragglers that might be hanging around to challenge healthy thinking, I continue for another minute or so by reciting a poem, singing a song, or rehearsing a talk I will be giving soon.

Depending on how often I have to stop and think to make sure I've remembered everything correctly (which, by the way, helps beat the competition), this entire effort only takes between 3 and 4 minutes. By now the unhealthy thought has been beaten to a pulp, and I stand alone on the playing field, triumphant. It is now time for the thunderous applause: I say to myself, "Good job. Well done!"

Another effective thought-stopping technique is the use of self-instruction. For example: "I know I'm not stupid. I might have erred, but I am not stupid!"

Finally, having vanquished my foe, I smile to myself. If I'm close to a mirror, I even smile at myself. I say, "Good job, Glenn. What a guy!" I will pat myself on the shoulder and stroke my arm from the shoulder to the wrist. I then describe to myself what I did that was so successful: "You immediately began thinking good, healthy thoughts, and you kept at it until you were completely free of your enemy. You amaze me, being able to remember all that at your age. I applaud you." (Which, by the way, I have done from time to time—when I'm alone, of course.) I don't even mention my enemy.

All this comes together into a powerful combination of positive verbal and physical reinforcement:

—"Good job, Glenn. What a guy!" (Positive verbal acknowledgment).

—I immediately began thinking good healthy thoughts about myself, and even saying them aloud (Descriptive praise). Research in verbal behavior has taught us that self-talk in the form of "self-regulation" (including self-instruction and self-reinforcement) revealed that "high levels of self-instruction corresponded with high levels of correct responding...and produced desired behavior change..." (Taylor and O'Reilly, 49).

—I pat myself on the shoulder, stroke my arm, smile, and even applaud myself. (Positive primary reinforcement that appeals to the senses of touch, sight, and hearing.)

To heighten the probability of success, I occasionally keep a record of my victories. (Behavior that is measured is behavior that is improved. That is basic to behavior therapy.) I give myself a point for every victory. After earning a predetermined number of points, I "spend" them on something I want very badly but can't have until I've earned—by behaving well—the required number of points. It's called "contingency management": Getting what I want is contingent on my doing what I'm supposed to do. It's a common theme in the teachings of Christ (Matt. 7:21–23. That's contingency management of the first order.). It is also called "Grandma's law": Eat your potatoes and carrots, and you will get pie and ice cream.

I recently earned 300 points for healthy thinking and spent them on a particular golf club I've been wanting for a long time. Shortly after earning that golf club, I played 18 holes of golf and was 3 under par on the first 9 holes and 2 under par on the second 9 holes. I even won the long drive contest: 328 yards! Not bad for a 62-year-old man who weighs 145 pounds! All the while I'm saying to myself, "See what wonderful things happen to you, Glenn, for behaving well." It's reinforcement that keeps on giving. It is intrinsic motivation shaped first by compelling extrinsic means.

Your reinforcers could be an item of clothing that enhances your appearance, and after earning it you would acknowledge that to yourself from time to time: "You look so nice in this. I'm so happy you behaved so well to get it. Good for you!" Presently, I am working on improving my behavior while driving. I have set my goal at 3,000 points, each point earned for behaving well. Once I earn the 3,000 points, I'll earn myself a particular car I want. At the time of this writing, I have earned nearly 2,200 points, and my behavior has improved remarkably. Even my wife has noticed and commented on it. (Now that's really reinforcing!) Furthermore, my improved behavior while driving has generalized to improved behavior in other settings. I am much more patient, for example, when I have to wait for others. It is really quite wonderful.

To make this self-improvement strategy work, there are a few things you must do. First, you must have a healthy incompatible behavior ready at an instant's notice. If you have to wonder what to do next, you're sacked by the competition and thrown for a loss. It's predictable. The instant the "problem thought" comes into your head, you have to be ready to push it aside to make way for the healthy behavior. It has to be something that is ready at hand: a song, a favorite quote, a mental exercise (e.g., naming all the states in the United States), and so on. Gandhi employed incompatible behaviors to carry him through tough times: "When doubts haunt me, when disappointments stare me in the face, and I see not one ray of light on the horizon, I turn to the Bhagavad Gita [a sacred book of Hinduism], and find a verse to comfort me; and I immediately begin to smile in the midst of overwhelming sorrow" (Fischer, 29).

Next, the healthy thought has to continue well beyond the passing of the unhealthy thought. If the unhealthy thought has only been pushed to the sidelines, it is too easy for it to come back to the playing field, sometimes more determined than before. Drive it away until it's out of the ball park, then lock the door behind it. This can take three to five minutes.

Then, acknowledge your success in some positive, reinforcing way. Do something good to yourself. Remember, behaving well must be more reinforcing than behaving badly.

Finally, introduce "solution thinking." Ask yourself, "What do I need to do to make things better?" "What must I know to do a better job parenting?" Then *act* on these by seeking out answers and putting them to work.

A beautiful example of rising above our sorrows and ending on a high note is found in Romans 7:17–25. Paul anguished over the "sin that dwelleth in me," causing him to lament, "O wretched man that I am! who shall deliver me from the body of this death?" Then he answered his own question and thanked "God through Jesus Christ." He overcame his problems Christ's way, which is the only sure way.

There is a great lesson here for parents who are grieving and anguishing over the behavior of their children. Parent as Christ would parent and be of good cheer.

Satan loves it when our countenance falls. He loves it when we droop, are down and dark. That's not Christ's way. His countenance is a joyous one (Acts 2:28).

If, as noted in Isaiah 3:9, our "countenance doth witness against" us, it can also witness for us. The question I ask you, therefore, is what does your countenance witness to your children? Does it shine upon them, or is it dark and foreboding. If it is the latter, then you must lift up your head and be of good cheer. Replace unhealthy introspection with healthy incompatible thoughts, then immediately reward yourself for such good behavior.

From time to time we all get down on ourselves. This should be the trigger that puts into motion a range of healthy responses that focus on solutions, not problems.

Lastly, a brief word about humor and "being of good cheer." Henry Drummond, in his classic little book *The Greatest Thing in the World*, wrote, "Christianity wants nothing so much in the world as sunny people" (77). I like that. No people on earth have a better reason to be sunny than do Christians.

An inextricable part of being "sunny" is humor. The two are yoked together. People love humor. In 1996, the most effective product advertisements in the world were the Eveready Energizer battery ads. And why? Because people found them to be the most humorous.

Study after study has revealed conclusively that the positive effects of humor are legion: reduced anger and defensiveness, relaxation, a clearer sense of perspective, a feeling of hope and hopefulness (Peterson, 17), and more. Here is something to lighten your day, while giving yourself something to think about:

> Anyone who imagines that bliss is normal is going to waste a lot of time running around shouting that he's been robbed. The fact is that most putts don't drop, most beef is tough, most children grow up to be just people, most successful marriages require a high degree of mutual toleration, most jobs are often more dull than otherwise. Life is like an old-time rail journey.... Delays, side tracks, smoke, dust, cinders, and jolts, interspersed only occasionally by beautiful vistas, and thrilling bursts of speed. The trick is to thank the Lord for letting you have the ride. (Jones, September 25, 1973)

Be of good cheer—for your children's sake and for your own. It's the better way to go!

Chapter Three

LO, I AM WITH YOU ALWAY

As I read both the popular and professional literature related to families and parenting, and as I work with parents and families who are experiencing serious problems, I notice that one distressing condition persists: Fragmentation! The glue that once held families together is losing its adhesive, bonding ability. What would Jesus do? I believe Christ would strengthen those family bonds with the glue of His presence. Throughout His ministry, He spent enormous periods of time *with His "children,"* teaching them, comforting them, leading them, strengthening them. Even at the end of His mortal ministry, when He would leave them and ascend into the heavens, He comforted them with this promise: "and, lo, I am with you *alway*, even unto the end of the world. Amen" (Matt. 28:20; emphasis added).

We need each other. "The Lord God said, It is not good that the man should be alone" (Gen. 2:18), and so He created Eve for Adam (and Adam for Eve) and commanded them to have children. No one is an island, and our physical, loving presence is especially important to our children. It gives them courage and strength.

When the Lord led the children of Israel out of Egypt, He "went before them by day in a pillar of a cloud,...and by night in a pillar of a fire, to give them light; to go by day and night" (Ex. 13:21). He never left them. On at least fourteen different occasions the Lord comforted one or many of His children with words like these: "Fear not: for I am *with thee*" (Isa. 43:5; emphasis added). Since He makes *us* safe with His presence, why shouldn't we make our children feel safe *with our presence*?

The Importance of Being with Our Families

And yet, gathering our families about us for instruction, recreation, and just plain togetherness is fast becoming a thing of the past. As noted by David and Roger Johnson, "Today, children are more isolated from parents, extended family members, and other adults than ever before.... The family, neighborhood, and community dynamics that once socialized young people into the norms of society are often extinct. Children [are too seldom being taught] how to manage conflicts constructively through example,...moral codes and patterns of living. Some communities directly promote violence as a way to resolve disputes" (3). The family, bound together in a Christian setting, can counteract those unhealthy influences. My wife and I have learned that convincingly.

While I was a graduate student completing the requirements for my doctoral degree, I found my role as a father being compromised. All six of our children were still home. We were barely making ends meet, and the need to complete my graduate work was overwhelming. The compelling matter of priorities was haunting us. It seemed that so many things were competing for the #1 spot. While attending church services one fall Sunday, across the pulpit came a message which put the matter of priorities at rest: family first! It was not an easy message to swallow or follow. But we did it, leaving one night a week, from 5:00 P.M. on, for nothing but family. Everything else stopped. All things considered, it seemed impossible, but we were reminded that "with God all things are possible" (Matt. 19:26). This decision provided a great opportunity for us to teach our children our values, to read the scriptures, to enjoy our children and to be enjoyed by them. We did it regularly, religiously, and in spite of occasional protests from the children:

—"Dad, do we have to? It's always so boring." (This despite the fact that Louise and I regularly went to great lengths to prepare enjoyable and substantive family activities.)

—"Can't I skip it tonight, Dad? I have so much home-work to do." (It was the only night of the week when home-work was ever mentioned as a priority!)

—"Let's make it quick, Dad. I've got a million important things to do." (Which meant watching a favorite TV show or bumming around with a friend.)

Occasionally, after an evening's activities, the children would say, "That was a good message" or "That was fun tonight."

As the years passed and our children began to leave home, we wondered what good had come from faithfully protecting these special evenings. I decided to ask our children. Their responses were astounding. Here is a sampling of what they said:

—"I particularly liked it when we discussed the life of Christ. I learned so much more than in Sunday School."

—"We had some really good times together: bowling, miniature golf, picnics in the canyon."

—"I liked it when we played charades and wrote down the things we liked about each other."

I probed deeper: "Is there anything else you remember about those evenings together as a family?" Again, the children only remembered pleasant, happy things:

—"Your lessons were always so good, Dad."

—"Those evenings straightened out a lot of messed up days and ended the day on a high."

Finally, after practically asking our oldest daughter to say it, she noted, casually and almost in passing, "Oh, sometimes we complained a little about them." I thought at the moment how strange it was that the complaining was what I remembered so much.

Despite those occasional complaints, we went forward with our weekly family activities, rarely if ever missing a night. Now, when we visit our children in their families, they too are faithfully holding their own family gatherings. As I reflect now upon ours, I too recall the good times, the wonderful times, the times to remember.

It is in retrospect that we have come to recognize those times together as the anchor that helped keep our family in place. Those nights became the most powerful teaching times of the week, far more powerful than anything that happened in church, Scouts, or youth meetings. Since it was an expectation the children had grown to respect, they knew where they were to be on those nights, and that's where they were. Of course, we did all we could to make being there a pleasant and happy experience.

A basic principle of human behavior teaches us that behavior is largely a product of the immediate environment. (Remember that!) What that means, simply, is that we behave differently in different environments because of what is expected of us in those different environments and the consequences which then follow our behavior. In a home environment where families do not do things together, children will behave in a vastly different way than children who grow up in a family environment replete with family activities and positive reinforcement for being involved. These activities can range from simply eating together at mealtime to taking vacations as a family.

Parents who correctly plan and carry out family activities create a home environment that teaches children things that can't be taught as well, or at all, in any other setting. In an environment filled with laughter, fun, and friendly competition, family members have an opportunity to talk to each other, cooperate, solve problems, practice positive roles, entertain, lead, follow, be responsible, say nice things, receive compliments, teach, be taught, participate, share—and the list goes on.

In such an environment, children view parents as leaders who are dependable, predictable, and safe to be around. An evening of closeness, fun, and sometimes intense interaction can set a positive tone for getting along for the rest of the week. Being together every week helps keep families together and on track. When NASA sends a spacecraft into orbit, midcourse corrections are constantly being made to keep the craft on target. NASA doesn't wait for days to see what happens and then say, "Oops, we missed" or "Good, we made it."

Family activities provide opportunities for subtle midcourse corrections that help keep us on target as a family. Looking back at our family activities together, I recall lots and lots of laughter, appropriate touching and hugging, intense listening and looking, and wonderful moments of just small talk. During friendly competition, winners would let out squeals of joy as they hugged their teammates. (Remember, the "teammates" were their brothers and sisters!) Jokes would bring uproarious laughter. Tears were shed as tender moments were shared. Questions were enthusiastically raised, followed by intense and engrossing discussions. Role playing brought out responses that left indelible impressions. I will remember forever the response of our oldest son during a role playing activity. I played the part of a schoolmate trying to talk him into doing drugs. As the pressure got more and more intense, I bore down hard on him and said, "What are you, a chicken?!" He looked at me silently for a few seconds, then answered, "Cock a doodle do." The family burst into laughter, and everyone learned a valuable lesson.

Guess what you would see if you could watch us together as a family today. That's right, lots and lots of laughter and happy times. Hugging and kissing, talking and listening. Sharing tender moments and shedding tears of joy and compassion. These are the fruits of togetherness. A friend of mine, the father of three children, noted, "Family nights make friends of family members!" Every week during family times together, children learn important lessons that can be learned in no other setting.

The Importance of Creating a Safe Home for Children

Among the many things science has taught us about high-risk and low-risk families is the need for parents to be safe for their children to be around. Safe from criticism, sarcasm, preaching, screaming, hitting, abuse (in any form), pleadings, and other "traps" parents get themselves into (Latham, 1996). Regularly gathering our family about us provides a powerful safeguard against circumstances that put families at risk.

Even so, a tradition of family togetherness does not mean children will never misbehave, get into trouble, do things they shouldn't do, and so on. What it does mean, however, is that the wrongdoing is less likely to alienate the child from the family. Rather, the family tends to pull together around the child, providing the care and compassionate support needed in times of crisis. This makes the family safe to be with, safe to come home to. As with the prodigal son, when such a child comes to himself, he will "arise and go to [his] father" (Luke 15:17–18).

On the other hand, high-risk families—those who have never learned to be close through laughter, touch, talk, listening, sharing, cooperating, and so on—tend to splinter even more in times of crisis, and whatever support system did exist is made that much weaker by the crisis. From such families, a comment typical of what I hear when, for example, a child has run amuck of the law is, "Let 'em put him away. He got what he deserved. We did everything we could, but he wouldn't listen. I really don't care if I ever see the kid again." The family becomes fractured, sometimes beyond any hope of mending.

Unfortunately, it is not unusual for parents to justify such a position in the name of religion. Dr. Larry Brendtro, a national leader in the effort to protect children, wrote, "I find it particularly ugly when retributive rationales are wrapped in religion to justify the decimation of our youth [on the basis that] 'He got what he deserved'" (Brendtro, "Mending Broken Spirits," 197–202). I suspect that's the kind of thing Paul was talking about when he cautioned the Corinthians about not "handling the word of God deceitfully" (2 Cor. 4:2), which is exactly what is done when the scriptures are used to justify coercive, abusive, punitive parenting!

Low-risk families, on the other hand, draw together in times of crisis. From such families I hear statements like, "We are sorry he did what he did. He'll have to pay for his mistakes, but we're ready to do what we can to help. We love him and we want him back."

Carefully planned and conducted family activities help parents create low-risk families in which people really care for one another. It is caring that grows little by little, activity by activity. Close relationships with safe, dependable, stable, "significant" people have been demonstrated conclusively time and again to be the tonic for troubled children and "a wounded nation"[1]

> If we peel away the decadent surface of our culture—the shootings and stabbings, assaults and rapes, murders, gang wars, and carjackings—underneath we find a wounded nation in terrible pain. Where there is violence, there is anger, and where there is anger, there is hurt. Our task is to heal this hurt through reconnecting youth with significant persons and helping them find new meaning in their lives. Relationships serve as a 'training ground' for learning how to be human. (Ponds, 217)

The importance of having that one "significant" person with whom to relate cannot be overstated. We are reminded of this fact by research on the effects that a "significant" person has on children of divorce. Those children who had achieved the most "wisdom and stability" were "always the ones who had at least one stable, responsible parent behind them all the way through" (Joselow and Joselow).

In my work with newlyweds and young parents, I am alarmed at the number of people who marry, often too young, to escape the unsafe environments of homes in which they were often the brunt of painful criticism, derision, screaming, threatening, coercion, and worse! These couples and young parents tend to be the ones who have the most difficulty adjusting to marriage and parenthood; they also struggle the most to establish in adulthood a healthy relationship with their parents. For them, going home for family visits is more an obligation than something they really want to do. A letter to Abigail Van Buren ("Daughter Feels She Can't Do Anything Right") illustrates the dilemma in which many young parents find themselves. The reader wrote:

---

[1] (For help and ideas with family activities, I recommend *Heritage Builders/Family Night Tool Chest, Book 1: an introduction to Family Nights*, and *Book 2: Basic Christian Beliefs*, by Jim Weidmann and Kurt Bruner, with Mike Nappa and Amy Nappa, available from Chariot Victor Publishing.)

Dear Abby:

Mother wonders why I enjoy spending so much time with my in-laws. Here are a few reasons:

My in-laws do not criticize me every time they see me. They don't say I look fat, my clothes are not appropriate or my hairstyle is out-dated. My in-laws don't point out everything I do wrong with my children; they say I'm doing a good job and should be proud of myself. Most of all, they listen when I talk.

Even though we live very close to [my parents] and see them often, I still feel like I'm a million miles away.

One longitudinal study found that by midlife, "children who ended up having the hardest time in life, who lacked emotional well-being, and who had a hard time in marriage, friendships, and even at work, were not necessarily the children of poor parents nor of rich parents nor even of obviously troubled parents. They were children whose parents were distant and cold and showed little or no affection" ("Harsh Words, Crushed Spirits," 4).

The importance of warm, human, parental attachment vs. material comforts is beautifully illustrated in an experience recalled by Mother Teresa. "Once I picked up a child [off the streets of Calcutta] and took him to our children's home, gave him a bath, clean clothes, everything, but after a day he ran away. He was found again...but again he ran away. [He] ran away a third time. [A sister followed him.] There under a tree was his mother. She had put two stones under a small earthenware vessel and was cooking something she had picked up from the dustbins. [The boy was asked], 'Why did you run from the home?' The child said, 'But this is my home because this is where my mother is'" (Spink, 72–73). You see, Mom and Dad, it doesn't take great skill, resources, or special training to connect with your kids. It takes you being with them in a loving setting. How simple can it get?

Our parenting is generational. That is, our children learn their parenting skills from us. Thus, the effects of our parenting are extended to our grandchildren and to their children. President Jimmy Carter, a devout Christian and dedicated family man, commented that he learned his "approach to the raising of children" from his father (78). He said, "In retrospect, I can see that instinctively emulating this autocratic father-son relationship a generation later was a mistake. Times had changed" (81). As Paul cautioned, "As your fathers did, so do ye" (Acts 7:51).

Parents, I plead with you to create a Christlike home that is safe for children of all ages. Say and do to your children only what you want done and said to your grandchildren. I call this my Golden Rule of parenting. (Another sobering thought: Be good to your children. They'll pick your nursing home!)

Following a talk I gave, a grandmother hurriedly approached me before I was able to leave the stand. She asked, haltingly, "Can you ever undo what you've done?" At that instant, even before I had time to answer, a young mother with a baby in her arms approached the stand. She looked up at this woman—her grandmother— and said, "Grandma, now you know why I scream at my kids," then walked away. The grandmother looked at me through the saddest eyes and said, "She's right, you know."

A recent letter reminded me of just how devastating and far-reaching coercive parenting is. The mother wrote: "I've been dealing with my children just like my father dealt with me. Angrily, verbally berating, criticizing—the list goes on. And I've hated myself for it—just like I hated him for it. I haven't spoken to him since I saw him at my wedding reception 12 years ago. And I've been turning into him. I can't let that happen. As I listen to the tone and voices of my children, I know I need to be a different parent. Now! So my children and grandchildren don't hear ugly voices!"

The following are examples of safe and unsafe parenting (Latham, *The Power of Positive Parenting*, 73–75). Safe parents are those who are approachable and nonjudgmental, parents who children want to be around and have around. Unsafe parents are parents whose children want to get away and stay away. Consider these scenarios, then ask yourself, am I safe or unsafe for my children?

Scenario #1: Defending a Friend

SAFE

Daughter: "I really feel bad for Helen. She's pregnant and her boyfriend doesn't want to have anything to do with her anymore."

Mom:	"She must really feel terrible. I'm certainly proud of you, Honey, for being so concerned."
Daughter:	"I don't know, Mom. It's so complex. But I'm going to keep being her friend."
Mom:	"Good for you. A true friend is worth more than gold, especially in situations like this. You're a good friend, Honey. I love you."
Daughter:	"I love you, Mom. It's so great talking to you—even about difficult things like this. You really understand."

UNSAFE

Daughter:	"I really feel bad for Helen. She's pregnant and her boyfriend doesn't want to have anything to do with her anymore."
Mom:	"Well, it was bound to happen. Play with fire and you get burned. I'm not the least bit surprised. She knew what she was getting into when she got mixed up with that loser. Just don't you get involved. It's her problem. Let her solve it."
Daughter:	"Mom! How can you say that? Helen's a neat girl. She just made a mistake. No one is perfect!"
Mom:	"Neat girls don't go to bed with dumb guys. You bet she made a mistake, and she'll pay for it the rest of her life. As for you, young lady, don't you dare do a stupid thing like that."
Daughter:	"I can't believe you, Mother!" (As she leaves in a huff).

Scenario #2:   Defending Himself

SAFE

Dad:	"That was quite a ball game last night. Your school really pulled it out of the fire in those last few minutes."
Son:	"Yeah. Squeaky, our point guard, was really hot."
Dad:	"That's for sure. And besides his ball handling skills, I understand he's a fine young man."
Son:	"He really is. He's in a couple of my classes and he's super friendly."

Dad: "The next time you see him, tell him what a great job I thought he did in that game."

Son: "I'll do that. He'll be happy to hear it."

Dad: "Let me know when the next ball game is. Maybe we can go together."

Son: "I'll do it, Dad. Sounds fun."

Dad: "I'll look forward to that."

Son: "Me, too. I gotta run, Dad. See ya."

Dad: "So long, Son. Have a good time. Take care. Love you."

Son: "Love you, too, Dad. See ya."

UNSAFE

Dad: "That was quite a ball game last night. Your school really pulled it o`ut of the fire in those last few minutes."

Son: "Yeah, Squeaky, our point guard, was really hot."

Dad: "That's for sure. And besides his ball handling skills, I understand he's an excellent student who hits the books like crazy every night. What kind of GPA does he have to maintain to stay on the team?"

Son: "He is a good student. I have some classes with him and he does well. He has to keep at least a C+ average to be on the team."

Dad: "I'm amazed he does so well with all of his athletic responsibilities. By the way, what's your GPA this year?"

Son: "I don't know for sure. Somewhere between a C and a C+."

Dad: "Now, Son, you can surely do better than that. Surely you have more time to study than Squeaky does. I mean with the amount of time you have, you should have a solid B average—or better!"

Son: "I'm doing all right in school. I'm passing. What's the big deal?"

Dad: "Just passing! I know you can do better than that. If a kid on the basketball team can do it, you can. You're just as smart as Squeaky."

Son: "Hey, what has Squeaky got to do with me? He lives his life and I live mine, and that's just how I want it!"

Dad: "I'll tell you what it's about. It's about your life. Without decent grades it's the end of school for you. Just look at Squeaky. I'll bet he not only gets accepted into college, but he'll get an athletic scholarship as well. He's got his head on straight. You could use a little of that head-on-straight stuff, young man!"

Son: "Forget it. I'm outta here. I don't need this crap."

Sparing the Rod

In their zeal to protect their children from themselves, parents often try to teach their children the important lessons of life using well-intended, but coercive, methods. In the two unsafe, how-not-to scenarios above, the parents' intentions were good, but what they did drove their children away: "She leaves in a huff." "Forget it. I'm outta here!" These are the fruits of coercion, a lesson taught to us convincingly by Dr. Murray Sidman in his epic book *Coercion and Its Fallout:* "Coercion encourages children to avoid, escape, and countercoerce" (meaning "get even") (78). That's what happened in the unsafe examples above. *The children escaped as quickly as they could!*

Christ would never coerce (force) his children to behave. Unfortunately, despite many others to the contrary, there are a few oft-quoted scriptures that suggest that coercion might be appropriate. Here are perhaps the two most frequently cited scriptures used to justify coercive parenting.

1. Proverbs 13:24 (See also 22:15, 23:13–14, 26:3). "He that spareth his rod hateth his son: but he that loveth him chasteneth him betimes." (Typically referred to as "spare the rod and spoil the child.")

The word *rod* has multiple meanings in and out of scripture. To a biblical shepherd, the rod was used to protect the sheep from the wolves. It was used for guiding the sheep. In Psalms, the rod is cited as a source of comfort: "Thy rod and thy staff they comfort me" (Ps. 23:4). It was used to separate the sheep from the goats. With its crook on the end, it was used to recover lambs from danger. In the book of Exodus (4:1–5), the "rod" is the authority of God, interpreted by some to also mean the word of God.

It is distressing that of the many positive uses and meanings of the "rod," humankind has chosen to focus on one punitive use: to beat up on kids. It is another sad example of how, over the ages, humankind has distorted good to justify evil. Once people become convinced that God is on their side, and that what they are doing is done in the name of God, anything is possible—including unspeakable carnage, savagery, horrors, and mayhem (Winner, 11A).

Among shepherds, the "rod" has a distinctly positive, functional, noncoercive meaning. Can you imagine Christ beating a child with a rod? Can you imagine Christ denying a child comfort?[2] I personally do not consider the beating of a child, in any manner or by any means, a Christian act. I can find absolutely nothing in the teachings of Christ that would condone such behavior. Nothing! It is a pre-Christian principle, fulfilled in Christ (Matt. 5:17), replaced with the Gospel of Love (Matt. 18:1–6).

Great care must be taken when generalizing from scripture to behavior. Consider this from Deuteronomy 21:18–21:

> If a man have a stubborn and rebellious son, which will not obey the voice of his father, or the voice of his mother, and that, when they have chastened him, will not hearken unto them:
>
> Then shall his father and his mother lay hold on him, and bring him out unto the elders of his city, and unto the gate of his place;
>
> And they shall say unto the elders of his city, This our son is stubborn and rebellious, he will not obey our voice; he is a glutton, and a drunkard.
>
> And all the men of his city shall stone him with stones, that he die: so shalt thou put evil away from among you; and all Israel shall hear, and fear.

And this one from Deuteronomy 22:21:

---

[2] For a magnificent treatment of the meaning of "the rod," I refer you to Phillip Keller's book *A Shepherd Looks at Psalms 23*, published in 1970 by Zondervan Publishers, Grand Rapids, Michigan.

Then they shall bring out the damsel to the door of her father's house, and the men of her city shall stone her with stones that she die: because she hath wrought folly in Israel, to play the whore in her father's house: so shalt thou put evil away from among you.

Remember, Jesus did not cast a stone at the woman caught in adultery, nor did He condemn her. Rather, He *counseled* her to "go, and sin no more" (John 8:11).

2. Matthew 21:12. "And Jesus went into the temple of God, and cast out all them that sold and bought in the temple, and overthrew the tables of the moneychangers, and the seats of them that sold doves."

Parents have cited this scripture to me as their excuse for expelling a wayward child from their home. I remind them that, in the first place, their home is not a temple of God—the temple served a different function than homes. I also remind them that access to the temple was limited to those who had met strict standards of behavior that qualified them to enter.

Comparing a home to a temple of God is a stretch. Children romp and play at home. They didn't romp and play in the temple. Family members lounge about in their pajamas at home. They didn't do that in the temple. Good people did many good things at home for which they would have been "cast out" of the temple. Home, no matter how good it is, is not a temple of God, nor does it have the same function.

We need to avoid simple comparisons which exploit the letter of the law while denying the spirit of it. We need to quit "handling the word of God deceitfully" (2 Cor. 4:2).

The frequent mention in scripture of so-called holy vengeance (e.g., Rom. 12:19—"vengeance is mine; I will repay, saith the Lord"), couched in chilling language (e.g. Rev. 6:8, 14:10–11, and 21:8), certainly creates an image of violent retribution—an angry God lashing back at his enemies. It is an image that is manifest across the face of the globe, seemingly irrespective of religious bearing or denomination. During a recent speaking engagement in China, my wife and I were taken to several religious shrines where the wrath of God was grotesquely displayed in statuary of people being tortured, torn, and tormented in the most hideous ways imaginable. In every instance, either a gloating god or a gleeful devil was approvingly looking on, an expression on their faces which said, "At last, you are getting what you deserve!"

I wish the writers of scripture would have used less violent language and imagery to portray the wages of sin. Regarding these polarized images of God—loving and merciful on the one hand, and full of wrath, anger, and vengeance on the other—I feel a deep kinship with Billy Graham who, in his autobiography, noted that when he gets to heaven he would like to engage God in a little Bible study about some of the seeming contradictions contained in it (Briggs, "Graham Looks Back," B1).

To me, the contrast between the tender, forgiving, patient, long-suffering, pure love of Christ and the wrath of an angry, vengeful, vicious, jealous God is one of those contradictions—at least seemingly so.

But in any respect, so far as parenting is concerned, there is no contradiction nor mixed message. Vengeance is not ours (Rom. 12:19). So put away the rod, and take upon yourself the image of Christ. As a parent, ask yourself what Paul asked the Corinthians: "What will ye? shall I come unto you with a rod, or in love, and the spirit of meekness?" (1 Cor. 4:21). The answer to that question is the same for you as it was for the Corinthians. It reminds me of a letter I got from the mother of a three-year-old girl. The mother wrote, "I cringe to think that I have asked the question, 'Would you like a spanking?' What a stupid question. What was she going to say? 'Sure, Mom, I love spankings. I'm a member of the young masochists club.'"

Before we can effectively teach our children what Christ would teach, we have to teach them *as* Christ would teach: gently, kindly, lovingly, patiently, persuasively, with long-suffering, not being easily provoked. We must literally be as Christ. When we teach that way, we are safe to be with. We are attractive to our children, and we attract them to us. Our words are believed, our actions are emulated, and our values tend to become their values. They begin to identify with us. It is a form of "modeling" which begins in infancy (Bijou, "Behavior Analysis," 96), involving the tendency of one variable to affect how another variable that has been associated with it is viewed. For example, if an ice cream cone tastes good to a child, and the color of the ice cream is red, the child will also come to like the color red. Conversely, if the ice cream cone tastes terrible and is red, the child will come to dislike the color red. It's called associative learning. There is a great message here for parents.

If parents harp at their children about cleaning their "filthy rooms," cleaning becomes associated with harping parents. So guess what happens to children's attitudes about cleaning and clean rooms? You are correct. Not only do they hate being harped at, they hate cleaning and they hate clean rooms. In my thirty plus years at this work, never yet has a parent told me, "I gave my son a severe tongue lashing about how he needs to clean out that filthy, stinking pig sty he lives in, and he said to me, 'You are absolutely right, Mother. It is a filthy, stinking pig sty. I'm so happy you brought that to my attention and made me aware of how important it is for me to keep my room spotlessly clean. I sense and appreciate your loving concern. I will clean it immediately, and you can be assured, it will stay that way.'" He will counter coerce. He will surely go off in a huff, more resolved than ever to keep his room a filthy, stinking pig sty and possibly make it even worse!

As parents, it is our responsibility to create a Christlike "world" in our homes, a safe place where children behave well because they enjoy the pleasant consequences of doing so, rather than to avoid the unpleasant consequences of behaving badly. It is a world in which a child thinks, "I know my parents will acknowledge and appreciate me," rather than thinking, "I'm only doing this to get my parents off my back," or "I am only doing this because I don't want to get beat on" (verbally or physically).

After giving a talk to parents on positive, noncoercive parenting, I got a letter from a young mother of four children. She told me of an experience she had with her five-year-old son soon after she returned home from hearing my talk:

> My five-year-old son and I were making cookies together. We were enjoying ourselves. We were almost finished so my

son asked if he could go play at his friend's house. I said, "You'll have to wash your face and hands and change your shirt first." He said, "No, Mom. I like this shirt. I'm going to wear this one."

I said, "If you want to go to your friend's, you'll need to change your shirt." (I was real calm, by the way.)

Then he said "no" again and exclaimed that the shirt he was wearing was fine. I calmly said, "I'm glad you understand what I expect of you, Son."

He said, "No I don't, Mom!"

I said, real cool, "I appreciate you understanding that I expect you to change your shirt."

He said, on his way out of the kitchen, "No, I won't."

He went to the bathroom, washed his face and hands and then went to his room. I calmly finished making the cookies. About a minute later, he emerged from the bedroom, stretched out his arms, and said, "There!" to show me that he had indeed changed his shirt. Amazing! I had really not much hope that he would change his shirt, and yet it worked. Like you said, "It works!"

Let's analyze this to understand *why* it worked.

First: The mother briefly stated her expectations in instructive rather than prohibitive language: she told the boy what he was to do, not what he wasn't to do. She said, "You'll have to wash your face and hands and change your shirt first," rather than, "You can't go until..."

Second: When the child protested and said, "No, Mom. I like this shirt. I'm going to wear this one," his mother did not become reactive and coercive: "Don't you say no to me, young man" (whap!). She remained "really calm" and briefly identified consequences while restating her expectations. "If you want to go...you need to change your shirt."

Third: The mother used empathy and understanding when the child objected again, while calmly repeating her directions: "I appreciate you understanding that I expect you to change your shirt, Son," then she left it at that. She created an environment safe from scoldings, threats, and force, and the child complied.

My studies reveal that 97 out of 100 times, when this approach is used, the child will comply—no matter what the age. Though the mother had little hope it would work, it did, and she was amazed. Doing things as Christ would do them, with love, with patience, without coercion, produces amazing results.

It Doesn't Take a Village

Much has been said about it taking an entire village to raise a child. This is a nice thought, but if parents leave it up to the "village" to raise their children, they are taking some terrible risks. Whether that village is the community, schools, church, social service agencies, law enforcement, or any other organization, they are all, at best, second-best substitutes for a good family and home environment. There isn't a shred of evidence to refute that.

The fact is, it doesn't take a whole village to effectively raise a child. It takes good parenting. Parents who turn their children over to the "village" to be raised are putting those children in harm's way. Over the years I have worked with many parents who have depended primarily on the village to raise and "fix" their children when they and their children were hurting: parents who, rather than read daily to their children, leave the teaching of reading entirely up to schools; parents who, rather than teach their children to manage their behavior well, leave that up to school personnel, church teachers and leaders, and law enforcement officials; and parents who turn the entertainment of their children over to the entertainment community. Schools, churches, and law enforcement are important, helpful parts of the village, but they are there only to support, enhance, and reinforce what parents should be doing at home. They are to supplement, not supplant, good parenting.

A whole village, working together toward common ends, can *help* raise a child. But that's the best it can do and the most it should be expected to do. As Vander Post and Taylor said: "[N]o culture has ever been able to provide a better shipyard for building storm proof vessels for the journey of man from the cradle to the grave than the individual nourished in a loving family" (130–31).

As parents, that means we must lovingly and patiently teach our children, for that is how Christ would do it. In fact, our very lives are our testimonies of what we teach. Centuries ago, Moses taught us that this is the way it ought to be: "And thou shalt teach [God's commandments] diligently unto thy children, and shalt talk of them when thou sittest in thine house, and when thou walkest by the way, and when thou liest down, and when thou risest up...

"And thou shalt write them upon the posts of thy house, and on thy gates" (Deut. 6:7, 9).

The Importance of Rewards

"People do what they do because of what happens to them when they do it" (Daniels, 25). This illustrates one of the basic principles explaining human behavior. Furthermore, the more instantly gratifying a behavior is, the more likely it is that that behavior will reoccur. "Immediate consequences...far outweigh...delayed and uncertain consequences" (Daniels, 31).

If our children continue to misbehave, regardless of what they have been taught, one can only conclude that the consequences of misbehaving are more desirable than the rewards of good behavior. That is why it is so important that parents are pleasant to be around and that they create a pleasant, safe, Christlike environment at home so children will be gratified for being there—and will want to be there rather than somewhere else.

Instruction, knowledge, understanding, attitude, and so on are only "antecedents"; the most they can hope to do is *get* a behavior going. Consequences *keep* behavior going, and if the consequences of children's behavior at home are punitive, or coercive, children are going to go somewhere else. It is a natural law of human behavior. Again, if children behave well at home only to avoid the negative consequences of behaving badly, rather than to enjoy the positive consequences of behaving well, as soon as they can, they will escape the home. You can count on it!

I am convinced, after decades of studying adolescent behavior, that the peer group, though powerful, gets more credit than it deserves for its ability to influence behavior. Certainly it has an influence, but in my experience that influence is, in great measure, correlated with the influence of the home. When home environments are coercive, unhealthy peer group influences tend to be heightened; when home environments are safe, unhealthy peer group influences tend to be lessened. As parents, we must quit blaming the peer group for all our children's inappropriate behaviors. Behavior begins at home!

A recent monumental study reported in the *Journal of the American Medical Association* (Resnick, et al., 823–32) found that parents have a powerful effect on their children's behavior all the way through high school. The study documented that though there is a perception among parents that once children enter adolescence, parental influence is surrendered to the peer group, "everything in the study suggests the contrary." "Throughout adolescence, parents remain absolutely central in the lives of kids," despite attempts on the kids' part to make it appear otherwise. The study discussed the importance of creating an "arena of comfort," a place where kids want to be and where there is a sense of belonging, of "connectedness."

I vividly recall a 15-year-old girl who up until her fifteenth birthday was everything a parent would want a child to be. As she approached 15, some things began going wrong in her life, and everyone, including her parents, reacted coercively. Rather than being kind, understanding, patient, and compassionate (i.e., Christlike), they became hostile, preachy, critical, threatening, and kept trying in vain to get through to her with reason and logic. The many good things about her—and there were many— were being ignored. Her teachers and parents came down on her like a ton of bricks because her A grades were slipping to Cs and Ds. Teachers openly ridiculed her in class. Several kids from her church shunned her and were verbally unkind. Her Sunday School class teacher became harsh and demanding. Her minister preached and preached and preached, warned and warned and warned. Before long home, school, and church became unsafe environments. Her "arena of comfort" was gone.

Simultaneously, a new group of schoolmates sought her out. They smiled and laughed with her. They were animated and "up." They took her in. The fact that they used alcohol, drugs, and tobacco and were living unhealthy lifestyles was now beside the point. To a rejected 15-year-old, they were safe. Guess where she went.

As sad as this was, things did not remain this way forever. The parents happily learned a better way, a Christlike way, and once they initiated a Christlike approach to parenting, things began to improve. Eventually, they made home into a safe place, a place of belonging, a place free of coercers (e.g., criticism, sarcasm, despair, pleadings, anger, threats, judgments, logic, reason, force), and the girl returned home to the family and its value system. The village did not effect that change; Christlike parenting did.

The following is an example of a noncoercive response that might have spared that child and her parents years of misery and regret.

Child: "I hate church. It's full of hypocrites. Even my Sunday School teacher came down on me in class today for something that wasn't even my fault. I'm never going back to that class again. NEVER!"

Parent: "Ouch! I can see why you're so upset. That would be tough for anyone to take. I appreciate your telling me about it, Honey. Can I help?"

Child: "Yeah. You can get off my case about going to church and let me lead my own life. At least I know where my friends are, and they aren't in church, I can tell you that. At school last week I met a guy from church and do you know what he said to me? He told me what a terrible person I am and then said some really mean things to me. Mom, that really hurt. I don't need that."

Parent: "That was cruel. It's hard to imagine that anyone would say something like that to anyone. But it's especially terrible when it's one of your classmates and church friends. I'm really sorry."

Child: "He's no friend of mine. I can't stand him. In fact, I can't stand any of them."

Parent: "Even friends sometimes say and do terrible things."

Note: No effort has been made by the parent to challenge the child's perception of things, nor was there any useless moralizing, preaching, logic, reason, or questions. Also, when the child said, "I can't stand any of them," she was overgeneralizing, a typical response from anyone who has been offended. Again, the parent didn't react with something like, "Well, now what about your friend Stacey? You don't really mean all of them, do you?" Remember this: behavior generalizes, and if in a moment of intense anger and frustration a child feels the need to make a point unequivocally, it is likely the child will take a very broad swipe at anything that even appears to challenge her position; e.g., "I already told you. I don't want anything to do with any of them!" And before long, the child is finding any number of reasons why she should dislike Stacey as well. The parent wisely chose to just listen empathetically and understandingly.

Child: "Mom, how could he have said such a thing? I just wanted to cry right there in school."

Parent: "It beats me. When I've been hurt like that, I've wondered the same thing. It's hard to know what gets into people to be so rude and unkind."

Note: The parent did not answer, or attempt to answer, the question. This is very important. In moments like this, the child is not looking for information. The child is seeking comfort and understanding. It would be very *unlikely* that an answer would result in the child saying, "Oh, I see what you mean. Because he is a stupid, insensitive jerk, that's what you can expect. I appreciate knowing that, Mom. Now everything is just fine. I can't wait to get back to church." That would never happen.

Also, the mother's response subtly lets the child know that she, too, has been the victim of such abuse. It can be very comforting to a child to know that someone else who is close has been badly treated but survived it.

Child: "Mom, I'm really confused. We are taught in church to be good and to be kind to one another. I see guys in church every Sunday who do things out of church that are really terrible. You can't imagine what it's like at school. Those so-called church going kids swear worse than anyone. What good is going to church?"

Parent: "It's sad, isn't it? It's the age-old problem of saying one thing then doing another. I only hope there are at least a few kids from church who stand up for what they are taught."

Child: "Oh, yeah. There are some. But one bad apple can sure ruin the whole bushel."

Note: With the momentum of the discussion moving in a safe, risk-free direction, there will soon be an opportunity to move away from the problem and toward a solution. It might go like this.

Parent: "I'm glad to hear that some of the kids are really good. You had me worried there for a moment. What should a person do when people who know better behave badly? I struggle with that all the time. The only thing I am really sure of is that I'm not going to let the bad behavior of others dictate how I behave!"

Child: "That's the hardest part of all, Mom. The first thing you feel like doing is getting as far away from them as you can get, even if it means not going to church. If there's anyplace you don't want to be with them, it's in Sunday School class!"

Parent: "You sure got that one right, Sweetie. I just try to be nice. I don't know what else to do. I figure that when it comes right down to it, I have to worry more about my behavior than about theirs. It's just a part of life. There will always be annoying, even disgusting people around. It's not a perfect world, for sure."

Child: "Mom, I know what you're driving at. You want me to keep going to church. But it's so hard when he's there. He's always bugging me, Mom. He looks at me and smirks. He always has this holier-than-thou look on his face. He thinks he's so righteous. He makes me want to barf. I hate him!"

Parent: "Honey, I don't want you to think I'm trying to preach to you or sneak some kind of lesson into this discussion. If it sounds like that, I'm sorry. Really, Honey, I struggle with this sort of thing just like you do. This isn't a problem faced just by kids."

Note:	Mom kept the air clear between her and her daughter while introducing one of the ugly realities of life: there will always be jerks and hypocrites around!
Child:	"Thanks, Mom. But I've got to think about this. I'm not going to drop off the deep end, but I need some time."
Parent:	"Fair enough. I hope it won't offend you if I tell you I'm also going to pray for you and invite you to do the same. Let's talk about it again in a few days. I love you."
Child:	"I appreciate that, Mom. I know you love me, and I love you."

This is not simply a script I made up out of thin air. It is a portrayal of scenarios I've helped hundreds of parents use, and the results have been, as one mother put it, "absolutely unbelievable!" It is an example of a safe parental response to a difficult and potentially dangerous situation, a response that is both scientifically sound and Christlike.

A mother who reviewed this manuscript before publication shared the preceding example with her husband and 20-year-old daughter. Here is an excerpt from a letter the mother wrote me about that experience: "After reading a few pages, I could tell my husband was not convinced the method or approach to the distraught teen was 'strong' enough. He commented, 'Well, that's certainly one approach.' It was then that our daughter in the back seat taught us both by saying: 'You don't know how many times I felt completely frustrated and boxed in during my high school years. Many times I would listen to your lectures, on the surface agree, and then complain the whole next day to my friends. I know now that what you were saying was right, but the fun and excitement, even acceptance, was with my boyfriend and friends...not at home. Dad, what Dr. Latham is saying is true.'"

If children continue to misbehave, it is for one or both of the following reasons:

1. Either they don't know how to behave as they should, or

2. They are being reinforced for behaving badly rather than being reinforced for behaving as they should.

Knowing this, our responsibilities as parents are completely clear:

1. Teach our children what behavior is expected of them, and
2. Make certain our children are positively recognized and reinforced within a safe environment for behaving as they have been taught and are expected to behave.

The Role of Religion

Now a word about the role of religion in child rearing. To Christian parents, participation in religious activities, church attendance, and belief in God and the religious teachings of their church are important—even highly valued. Here are a few thoughts and suggestions about those matters for your consideration.

1. There is little or no evidence to suggest that dogma (that is, denominational doctrine) has much effect on the moral behavior of children. Writing on the topic "Children and Religion," Harriet Cobb noted that "exhaustive studies indicate no significant relationship between the two; that is, denomination dogma and children's moral behavior. To children, denomination is but a name which becomes associated with its characteristic rituals" (480).

You can bet your bottom dollar that the majority of the 4,000 murders a year committed by kids are committed by kids who knew it was morally wrong to do so. And so it is with the mounting cases of rape and sexual molestation, robbing, cheating, lying. A number of these crimes were and are committed by *kids of various religious denominations* who all know that the doctrines of their respective religions forbid such behavior. But they do it anyway. Why?

They do it, as has been pointed out in some detail above and in chapter 2, because it is more immediately reinforcing to behave as they shouldn't than it is to behave as they should.

2. Parents historically tend to coerce children by threatening them with the "fear of God." Again, quoting Harriet Cobb, "Parents who frequently use the threat that 'God will punish' to ensure compliance in their children tend to punish their children more frequently than parents who do not form an alliance with a punitive God" (480–81). And with what result? Countercoercion! Such threatened children do exactly the opposite of what they are supposed to do just to get even with their parents or with the coercive, punitive culture that is attempting to force compliance. Such countercoercive behavior produces a sense of power and control, and that is much more reinforcing than is a feeling of subjugation. You can count on it.

3. Punitive, coercive religious doctrines have a demeaning effect on youth. Despite what we know about "the importance of developing a positive self-concept in children," religious doctrines which "espouse a belief in the 'evil nature' of humankind" actually lower self-esteem and reinforce feelings of guilt (Cobb, 481), neither of which bodes well for healthy behavior.

4. "Youth with absent or abusive fathers may...have trouble with a God called Father. Fathers create life, and their role is to provide for, nurture, and protect their children. Why should one trust a Father God without ever having trusted an earthly father?" (Harris, 22–23).

5. Religious teachings tend to become believed and valued— when they are taught lovingly in action and in deed. There is certainly nothing new here. How often have we heard it said, "I'd rather see a sermon any day than hear one."

Happy, meaningful, active, positive involvement in the religious or church community is what produces Christlike behavior, not dogma. This means enticing children toward service to others and to the community, giving rather than receiving, sacrificing for others, involvement in caring relationships, volunteerism—in other words, what I choose to call participatory religion (Benard, 29–32; Werner and Smith).

Parents, if you want your children to believe like Christians, get them behaving like Christians. Attempting to beat the devil out of them or threatening the fear of God into them isn't going to do it. It never has and it never will. Nor is simply attending church going to do it. As the early twentieth-century evangelist Billy Sunday reminded his listeners, "Going to church doesn't make you a Christian anymore than going to a garage makes you a car!"

6. Religious beliefs, well taught through modeling and practice, ultimately become active spiritual values rather than simply dogma, and children's lives are better for it. They are more virtuous and morally clean, are less likely to be involved in substance abuse, and are more law-abiding with lower rates of juvenile delinquency and violence (Benson, "Religion").

In other words, when spiritual and religious values and teachings are appropriately applied, children's lives are more likely to be happy and productive. As noted by Peter Benson, a leader in practical research on issues related to values and youth, "It is apparent that a spark of spiritual or religious connection is present in the lives of a majority of adolescents,...[but since] spirituality is the least understood of human capacities...it is the least nurtured" ("Spirituality," 209). "To the extent that religious institutions emphasize creed to the exclusion of nurturing spiritual capacity, too often they push adolescents away—not only from that particular faith, but from the spiritual quest itself... [T]he common approach of religious indoctrination often stifles the spiritual, leading too frequently to the abandonment of both spirituality and meaningful engagement with a specific religious tradition" (219).

If parents will be more Christlike, religious and spiritual involvement will be sweet, and our "little ones" will be far less likely to perish.

Chapter Four

REVILE NOT

To the Corinthians, Paul spoke plainly. He reminded them, "Know ye not that the unrighteous shall not inherit the kingdom of God?" And then he named revilers as unrighteous, along with fornicators, idolaters, and abusers (1 Cor. 6:9–10). To not revile is a Christlike virtue, as taught to us by Peter, who wrote, "When [Christ] was reviled, [He] reviled not again; when he suffered, he threatened not" (1 Pet. 2:23).

Is it any wonder that reviling would be ranked with such behaviors as fornication, idolatry, abuse, theft, covetousness, drunkenness, and extortion? Think about it in light of some of the very worst problems in the world today: Protestants reviling against Catholics, and Catholics reviling against Protestants in Ireland; Palestinians reviling against Israelis, and Israelis reviling against Palestinians in the Holy Land; Christians reviling against Muslims, and Muslims reviling against Christians in Yugoslavia, and on and on. What is even more astounding is that all of this reviling is going on in the name of religion—much of it even in the name of Christianity, despite that doctrine which is as basic to true Christianity as any of its doctrines: "Love your enemies, bless them that curse you, do good to them that hate you, and pray for them which despitefully use you, and persecute you" (Matt. 5:44).

Christ is the perfect example of nonreviling, even in the face of cruel and unwarranted assaults; in circumstances where he was spit upon, buffeted, smitten, taunted, rejected and denied, mocked and even crucified (Matt. 26:67–70 and 27:29, 35), he did not revile. He did not strike back. Though he could have called down "more than twelve legions of angels" (Matt. 26:53), he "reviled not." He was a frequent, almost continual, victim of reviling from the very beginning to the very end of His life, even by those who suffered with Him: "And they that were crucified with him reviled him" (Mark 15:32). An old Yiddish saying goes, "If God lived on earth, people would knock all his windows out" (Rosten, 4). The more supreme the goodness, the more it seems to attract revilers— and the less it seems to revile in return. This is the model parents should emulate when being buffeted about by unruly children. Revile not!

While working with families with persistent problems between parents and their children, I have found that without exception, virtually everyone is in some way reviling against someone. A child screams and parents scream back. A child hits another child and the parents hit the hitter. Reviling against revilers. Responding in kind. A mother told me of how her year-old baby bit her on the cheek and how she bit the baby back: "I needed to teach her that biting hurts," the mother said. True, the mother needs to teach the child not to bite, but biting back is not the way to do it. That's reviling. The better way, the proper way, would be to gently put the child down and just walk away without saying a word. My research has revealed conclusively that it would take only a few responses of this kind and the biting would stop. No scolding, no hitting, no shouting, no biting—just walk away.

The results are amazing! Why has the violence in South Africa between blacks and whites taken such a marvelous and dramatic decline? I'll tell you why. It's because Archbishop Desmond Tutu, a black, said it is time to stop. And who stopped first? The blacks! Those who for decades suffered "the killing and torture" by the whites (*USA Today*, Oct. 15, 1997). Does that give you some clue as to what it means to be Christlike?

When parents calmly walk away from such negative behavior, they deprive the child of the thing the child wants most: parental attention. Parental attention is *the most powerful* force or consequence in the shaping of children's behavior. When attention is not forthcoming, the behavior is less likely to be repeated.

If a parent is consistent, the child will soon learn that parental attention is available only when the child behaves appropriately. As a result, the inappropriate behavior is soon extinguished. Like a fire without fuel, it goes out.

When children behave in ways that parents find objectionable, I typically hear moms and dads ask despairingly, "What is going on inside that kid's head?" They envision some little monster gene rampaging wildly through the kid's psyche, whipping up all kinds of mischief. Not so. It is not what's going on inside the child that explains behavior. It is what is going on *outside* or *around* the child that explains the behavior. The sooner parents learn that and respond accordingly, the sooner their parenting skills will improve.

Webster defines *reviling* as "to use abusive language." A synonym of *revile* is *scold*. To "revile not" means not using abusive language against those that use abusive language with you, or to not scold those who scold you.

Scolding is defined as "noisy quarreling; angrily and noisily finding fault, rebuking, berating in irritation or ill temper, prolonged and continuous berating." *Berating* is defined as "condemning vehemently and at length." *Vehement* means "intense, emotional, bitter." Furthermore, a reviler is one who despises.

By any definition, reviling is contrary to Christlike behavior in any setting. When asked by Pilate, "Hearest thou not how many things they witness against thee?" Christ "answered him...never a word; insomuch that [Pilate] marveled greatly" (Matthew 27:13–14). Christ responded with silence when revilers blindfolded him, struck him in the face, then asked mockingly, "Prophesy, who is it that smote thee?" (Luke 22:63–64). Similarly, when the high priest challenged him, "Answerest thou nothing?

what is it which these witness against thee?...Jesus held his peace" (Matt. 26:62–63).

Later, when the elders, chief priests, and scribes asked him, "Art thou the Christ?" he answered simply, "If I tell you, ye will not believe: And if I also ask you, ye will not answer me, nor let me go" (Luke 22:67–68). His answer was brief, not prolonged or contentious as is typically characteristic of revilers. He was not intense, emotional, or bitter.

Christ's life was one of not reviling. Isaiah prophesied of it: "He is despised and rejected of men; a man of sorrows, and acquainted with grief...he hath borne our griefs, and carried our sorrows,...was wounded for our transgressions,...bruised for our iniquities,...oppressed...and...afflicted, *yet he opened not his mouth*" (Isa. 53:3–7; emphasis added).

Counsel against reviling is among the most prominent of Christ's messages to us. Here are but a few examples:

Proverbs 15:1 "A soft answer turneth away wrath; but grievous words stir up anger."

Proverbs 16:32 "He that is slow to anger is better than the mighty..."

Matthew 5:9 "Blessed are the peacemakers: for they shall be called the children of God."

Matthew 5:39 "...whosoever shall smite thee on thy right check, turn to him the other also."

Matthew 5:40 "And if any man will...take away thy coat, let him have thy cloak also."

Luke 6:28 "Bless them that curse you, and pray for them which despitefully use you."

1 Corinthians 13:4–8 "Charity suffereth long,...is not easily provoked...Beareth all things..."

Romans 12:14 "Bless them which persecute you: bless, and curse not."

Romans 12:17 "Recompense to no man evil for evil."

Given the importance of not reviling in our interactions with others outside the home, think how doubly important it is that we not revile inside the home. Remember, reviling includes:

Definitions	Examples
Abusive language	Swearing, name calling, criticism, sarcasm, vituperation.
Scolding	"Chewing out," noisy quarreling, anger, noisy fault finding, prolonged and continuous rebuking.
Berating	Condemning vehemently, intensely, emotionally, bitterly.

These are contentious, satanic tools for tearing families apart. Christ instructs us through Paul that we must be "gentle unto all men, apt to teach, patient. In meekness instructing those that oppose themselves...that they may recover themselves out of the snare of the devil" (2 Tim. 2:24–26). And no satanic snare is more insidious than is reviling. It's one of his devices.

Reviling invariably leads to problems. Nonreviling puts problems to rest, leaving us clear of fault. Christ's encounter with Satan is a classic example of this. Each temptation was followed by a nonreviling response, until at last defeated, the devil left and "angels came and ministered unto [Christ]" (Matt. 4:4–11).

There is another great lesson for parents in this contest between Christ and Satan. Christ only had to be direct with Satan three times. There is something instructive here. In my research on the treatment of behavior problems, I have been astounded to find that if parents remain calm, empathetic, and direct even in the face of outrageous reviling, 97 out of 100 times, on the third directive, children will comply. I have demonstrated this in role-playing situations to audiences all over the world, and parents are utterly amazed at how the person playing the reviling child, even in a role-playing setting "just run[s] out of gas"—as one parent put it—after three times. It is reminiscent of a thought credited to Thomas Jefferson: "Nothing gives one person so much advantage over another as to remain always cool and unruffled under all circumstances."

Occasionally I am called upon by high school teachers to talk to their students about how to manage their own behavior. Recently I was in a classroom at an alternative high school. During the visit, I was explaining to the students how important it is to create our own environments so that we are reinforced more often for behaving appropriately than for behaving inappropriately. I was trying to convince the students how much better it is to be self-managed than to be controlled by parents who use the punitive, negative, coercive measures with which many of the students were all too familiar.

The discussion turned to their impending roles as parents and what they could do to create in their homes nonpunitive, noncoercive, nonreviling environments where their children would feel safe and be reinforced for behaving well rather than punished for behaving inappropriately. Referring frequently to the science of human behavior, I was anxious for the students to understand that the best way to teach children to behave well is to positively acknowledge their "good" behavior, while pointing out that the worst way to induce children to behave well is to respond negatively to their inappropriate behavior. Shouting, spanking, threatening, squeezing, and so on are needlessly negative and produce resentment and rebellion in children.

At this point, a lanky, fair-haired boy, with doubt written all over his face, raised his hand and said, "That's crazy! The only way you keep kids in line is to beat it into them. If my old man didn't let me have it when I'm acting up (and he slammed his clinched fist into the palm of his hand), I wouldn't be here in this alternative high school. I'd be in jail." He then went on to describe in some detail the coercive, punitive methods his father used to keep him "in line." I asked the boy if he would be willing to role-play with me a different way of managing inappropriate behavior, a nonreviling way. He agreed.

When he stood up, I was immediately impressed with how tall he was. He literally towered over me. I told him I wanted him to behave exactly as a boy his age and disposition would behave when he had a serious disagreement with his father. I encouraged him not to hold back simply because I was this little old fellow for whom he might feel some sympathy or even respect. I asked him to "let it all hang out." We created a scenario which involved a serious disagreement between me, as the father, and him.

Taking my advice to heart, he let me have it, assaulting me with every profane, verbally distasteful, vituperative expression imaginable. I stood there calm and composed while he vented all over me, and then I said, "I can tell you're very upset about this, Son. I suspect I might be also under the circumstances." Again, he verbally lashed out at me. By now the eyes of everyone in the class were riveted on us. With the exception of the boy's tirade, the room was quiet and still. Again, being fully composed, I looked deep into his eyes and said, "Son, I'm really sorry this has upset you so much." Sensing that he was calming down and relaxing, I reached out, gently patted him on the shoulder, and said, "Son, even though you are terribly upset, and perhaps for good reason, what would be a more mature way for you to manage your own behavior in a situation like this?"

Silence hung heavy in the classroom. The boy's anger drained from his face. His eyes, which only moments before were filled with fire, became almost dim. Even the color left his face. He stood there for several seconds just looking down at me; then with a voice that could barely be heard, he said, "You know, that would work with me." On the third time, he complied. It worked! Indeed, "a soft answer turneth away wrath" (Prov. 15:1).

Reading the scriptures, I am amazed at how often efforts, instructions, queries, and events meant to achieve important ends or to deliver significant messages came in groups of three:

1 Samuel 3:4–8 The Lord called Samuel three times.
Matthew 4:3–10 Christ refused Satan's temptations three times.
Matthew 12:40 Jonah was three days in the belly of the whale as was the Son of man in the heart of the earth.
Matthew 26:40–48 Christ woke His sleeping disciples three times in Gethsemane.
Matthew 26:69–75 Peter denied Christ three times.
Matthew 27:63 Christ rose from the tomb after three days.

John 21:14 Jesus showed Himself to His disciples three times after His resurrection.

John 21:15–17 Jesus asked Peter three times, "Lovest thou me?"

Acts 9:8 For three days, Paul was without sight and neither ate nor drank.

Acts 10:15–16 The Lord told Peter thrice that he was to not call unclean that which God had cleansed.

2 Corinthians 12:7–8 Paul sought the Lord thrice to remove the thorn from his flesh.

1 John 5:7–8 There are three that bear record in heaven and in earth.

Whether I am stretching a point, I don't know. But I do know that during a family tempest, parents who will follow the example of Christ in His confrontation with Satan are most likely to still the tempest quickly and begin bonding with their child. The following scenario illustrates a nonreviling approach to dealing with a tempest in a household. As you read this, remember that empathy, understanding, directness, and nonreviling are the keys.

Setting: A mother is clarifying her expectations regarding her daughter's use of the family car.

Mary: "Mom! This is crazy. I know how to take care of myself and the car. I really resent this!"

Mother: "Mary, I can appreciate that you might find this a little annoying. I'm sorry it upsets you, but this is super important to me. Now, think about it, what would you do if your friends began pressuring you to do something really inappropriate like drag racing with the car? Kids do that sort of thing—especially if it's someone else's car!"

Mary: "I resent being treated like a baby!"

Mother: "I still need to know what you'd do in the face of peer pressure, because you will certainly face it sooner or later."

Mary: (A bit disgusted!) "Oh, for heaven's sake, Mother. I'd just tell them no. I'm no dummy. I'd just tell them I'm not going to do a stupid thing like that!"

Mother: "Thanks, Mary. That assurance means a lot to me. Knowing what I can expect from you in a moment of crisis is very important and your response is very comforting."

Note: You'll notice how the child tried to draw the mother off track, but she wouldn't allow that to happen. The mother completely ignored any mention of how "crazy" her concern was, how annoyed or offended the girl was, or how "nonadult" the girl was being treated.

The mother didn't revile by arguing, becoming upset, preaching, moralizing, resorting to logic or reason, or any similar approach. With compassion and understanding ("I can appreciate that you might find this a little annoying. I'm sorry it upsets you..."), she directly pressed her need for the required information ("...but this is super important to me"). Though the girl resisted and balked twice, on the third time she finally came forth with an acceptable response. This is quite predictable.

If parents remain proactive and on course, the chances are overwhelming that the child will come forth with an acceptable response. On the way there, the child might be sullen, angry, disgusted, or caught up in any number of resistive behaviors. Just let it go. Respond as a highly civilized adult no matter how uncivilized the child behaves. Why should you get upset? After all, it's your car. You can use it whenever you wish.

Suppose that after three directives for a response, the child gets so upset she simply won't cooperate. Just say:

Mother: "Mary, I can see you are really upset by this conversation. Let's drop it for now and revisit it again *when you are more in control of your emotions*. Once we have finished our conversation, the privilege of using the car will be yours."

Note: The complete responsibility for the positive resolution of the problem is right where it should be—on the child's shoulders. The parent has not tried to resolve the problem at a moment of emotional upset. Never attempt resolution when a person is drunk, stoned, emotionally enraged, or distraught! Wait until they sober up, dry out, or calm down. That is a nonreviling way of responding.

Let's suppose that Mary really comes unglued:

Mary: (Shouting) "What? Do you mean to tell me that I can't use the car until I've answered your stupid, lousy, [!@#$%^&*] questions? I need the car, Mother, and I need it tonight. I have plans! I've passed Driver's Ed, I passed my driver's test, and I have my license. You have no right to do this to me, Mother! No right at all! I can't believe this!" (huff, puff)

Mother: (Calmly) "Mary, as soon as we've finished this discussion and I have the assurances I need, the privilege of using the car will be yours. It's up to you. Go to your room, cool down, think it over, then let's resume this discussion when you are ready to do so calmly."

Note: Mother has not been drawn off course or allowed the daughter's rage to enrage her. She did not revile against her reviler. Mother has not been distracted by profanity (which might well be discussed later) and has reminded her daughter that using the car is a privilege, not a right! She quietly and simply gave direction to the girl's behavior and with that gave her the responsibility for the ultimate resolution of the problem: "Go to your room, cool down, think it over, then let's resume this discussion when you are ready to do so." By proceeding this way from the beginning, though the responses sometimes become distasteful and clouded with emotion, the child will soon come around. After all, you are managing a very powerful contingency. It usually proceeds something like this:

Setting: The girl returns and, though outwardly calm, is still upset. Mother has a faint, though compassionate smile on her face. (Not a smirk!) She is in complete control. The daughter is likely a bit confused by this. Only a short time earlier she had pulled out all the stops in an effort to blow her mother away, but Mother is still there, well anchored, in complete control, unmoved, unruffled. By now the daughter must certainly be thinking, "What a brick!" She composes herself; she postures herself to be equal to the task.

Mary: "Mother, I'm sorry you don't trust me. I feel like you are
           treating me like a baby. As you can tell, that really upsets
           me. Still, it is obvious to me that I'm going to have to
           endure this little charade of yours before you're going to
           let me use the car. So let's get this over with!"

Note: What an astounding victory for mother and daughter!
           The mother's strength as a calm and in-control leader in
           the home has been established, and even though the
           daughter (typically) doesn't appear to like it, she respects
           it, and at that age respect is more meaningful than love.
           Children of that age understand respect a lot better than
           they understand love, let me tell you! In time, under such
           conditions, both love and respect will emerge.

Mother: "Thanks, Honey. I'm glad you're ready to proceed. Now,
           getting back to where we left off..."

Note: Mother cut through all the verbal smog and got right
           back on task. She was directive rather than reactive.

Strategies like this relieve us of the fears that conflicts
between us and our children will go on forever. They don't. I have
yet to document an inflamed difference of opinion to persist more
than a few minutes when the situation is handled with empathy,
understanding, and directness—all of which are nonreviling.
Differences of opinion might continue, but the flames are out.

I regard verbal reviling as the number one enemy to good
parent-child relationships. We are always looking for that gold-
en thought, the Teflon-coated message that will pierce the thick
skulls of our children and enlighten their minds. Baloney! What
typically happens is that an emotional conversation surrounding
substantial differences explodes, battle lines are drawn, positions
get defended and become even more polarized, and the war is on:

Setting: The daughter comes home from school an hour and a
           half late.

Mother: "Where have you been, Mary? Out with that obnoxious
           bunch of kids again, I suppose. How long will it take
           before you learn what a bunch of losers those kids are!?"

Mary:	"Leave my friends alone. Who I run around with is none of your business. You've got some friends that make me as sick as mine do you."
Mother:	"Just leave my friends out of this. You might not like them, but at least they are responsible people. I don't need to be ashamed of being seen with them!"
Mary:	"Hah! I wouldn't be caught dead with that bunch of old fogies!"
Mother:	"Hang around with your bunch of losers and you'll be dead."
Mary:	"Believe me, there are things worse than death. Living in this crummy house is one of them"
Mother:	"You unappreciative brat! To think of all I do to provide for you and this is the thanks I get. Why do I even bother!?"
Mary:	"You don't need to bother anymore. I'm out of here!" (as she slams the door behind her)

Countenances fall, and angry, spiteful, sinister, destructive things follow. The environment in the home becomes coercive, and the child is gone, complicating any efforts at reconciliation.

To see the contrast, you might want to read again the account of the mother's nonreviling response to a terribly angry 16-year-old daughter with which I began this book. It is a beautiful and true example of the fruits of nonreviling parenting, Christlike parenting. In that example, the mother was empathetic, understanding, but direct. Furthermore, she carefully selected out of all the junk thrown at her the one thing worth attending to: the fact that the daughter knew she was expected to vacuum the floor. The mother did not revile; rather, she began restructuring the environment into a healthier, more positive, facilitative environment.

I appreciate the wisdom found in Proverbs 29:11: "A fool uttereth all his mind: but a wise man keepeth it in."

Parents and Punishment

Volumes have been written in both the professional and the popular literature about the bitter fruits borne of parents who revile. The biographies of Adolf Hitler, Joseph Stalin, Mao Tse-tung, Saddam Hussein, and Slobodan Milosevic, five of this century's notorious despots, are accounts of men who grew up in abusive, reviling environments where anger and hatred were learned early, then viciously and continuously acted out over prolonged periods. Studies of parent-child relationships remind us of this: Parents of [misbehaving] children have a firm belief that the harsher the punishment, the more likely it is that the child will remember it and that it will be effective. Such parents were often exposed to harsh punishment themselves and tend to replicate it with their own children" (Walker, Calvin, & Ramsay, 363).

Dr. John Reid of the Oregon Social Learning Center in Eugene, Oregon, a national authority on violence and antisocial behavior, spoke to a group of educators in Washington, D. C. The topic was violence in homes and schools. He noted that the two variables most closely linked to violence were "harsh, abusive, emotional discipline" and "the lack of supervision." He further noted that the keys to preventing and treating violence are "clear, reasonable, age-appropriate expectations," "positive and consistent discipline techniques," and "supervision of children, including knowing their whereabouts" (June 12, 1995).

Parents who revile and use aversive, punitive means for managing their children's annoying, inappropriate behaviors typically do so because they want instant compliance—and they often get it. But in the long run, it turns out to be a bad trade of short-term gains for long-term losses.

Nearly without exception, the origins of violence are found in violent parent-child relationships where the emphasis is on punishment rather than teaching, expediency rather than growth. As noted by a UC Irvine graduate student in his study of the teen/parent relationship: "Children act like the adults who raise them" (Smith, 5). Bill Moyers cited a report of the American Psychological Association which traced the origins of violence to parental abuse and harsh physical discipline: "Children learn violence at home, and the lessons are reinforced by the glorification of violence in the media, which treats cruelty and death as entertainment for profit" (4–5). A recent study on the origins of youth violence, reported at a professional conference, revealed that 43%

of that violence had its origins in what kids saw on TV, and 27% had its origins in violent parenting behavior. Can you imagine that! Seventy percent of all youth violence is rooted in what is taking place within the walls of our own homes! Folks, if you don't get the parenting message from this, read and reread it until you do!

On August 28, 1997, CNN reported the death of prominent TV executive Brandon Tartikoff. During the report, an earlier recorded "clip" of Mr. Tartikoff was aired during which he reminded TV producers of their responsibility for what is shown on TV because "television is a medium that encourages imitation." Truer words were never spoken. In that same CNN report, it was noted that, on the average, children view 25 acts of violence for every half hour of TV they watch.

A colleague of mine noted, "We have a passion to punish," to which I add "and an aversion to teach." I was once asked to give a talk to a group of preschool teachers. On the program was attached this note: "Children are like nails. When they are bent out of shape, a pat on the back will straighten them out better than a thump on the head." How true.

Spanking, hitting, squeezing, and screaming at children to force compliance or to punish them for misbehavior has got to stop! Research conducted by Dr. Nathan Blum, a pediatrician with the Division of Child Development and Rehabilitation, University of Pennsylvania School of Medicine, has documented that "shouting excites youngsters so they actually misbehave more" (A6).

Maybe this will put the problem into perspective. If you don't want your grandchildren screamed at and hit, don't scream at and hit your children. If you don't want to be neglected or abused in your old age, don't neglect or abuse your children today. In 1996 there were 300,000 cases of elder abuse reported in America. A large percentage of that abuse was inflicted by the children of those parents (*Eye on America*). Evidence is emerging that children abused by their parents become abusive to those parents in their old age. As observed by a juvenile court judge presiding over a case involving a girl who beat her father to death with a baseball bat after suffering years of physical abuse, "If there is a lesson to be learned from this, it's that if you mess with your kids enough, they're going to beat your brains in" (*Newsweek*, 21).

What parents have simply got to understand is that reviling, whether in the form of hitting or shouting or threatening, only weakens their position, while strengthening the child's. Writing of India's struggle for independence, Louis Fischer pointed out that under Gandhi's leadership "the British beat the Indians with batons and rifle butts. The Indians neither cringed nor complained nor retreated. That made England powerless and India invincible" (275). No wonder an observer referred to Gandhi as the most Christlike person he ever knew.

A few years ago, a concerned mother and her 14-year-old son came to see me. The boy had been harassed badly by a neighborhood bully, and it was beginning to affect how he felt about himself. The boy's father and grandfather advised the boy to strike back: "Don't let him push you around. Let him know you can defend yourself!" Happily neither the boy nor his mother felt this was the thing to do, so they came to see me. I made a number of suggestions, all of a proactive, nonreviling nature. When they left, I felt impressed to write the boy a letter to emphasize what I had suggested. I said, "If you can lead with love and compassion rather than retaliate with anger and revenge, I am sure you will win great victories in life. Abraham Lincoln was criticized by one of his associates because he went out of his way to make friends of his enemies. His associates asked President Lincoln, 'Why don't you destroy your enemies rather than make friends of them?' Lincoln answered, 'Don't I destroy my enemies when I make friends of them?'

"Pattern your life after the lives of great men and women. Don't allow your image of yourself to be shaped by these immature and unkind behaviors of a confused and unhappy neighbor boy."

And you know what? It worked! In fact, he has shaped, for good, the behavior of the bully. He destroyed an enemy by making him a friend. Like Lincoln, like Gandhi, and like Christ, he won. In fact, everyone won!

From a summary of research on the origins of antisocial behavior as reflected upon by youth and adults in lockup facilities and correctional institutions, I can document six major complaints about the parenting they received. One of them relates to our discussion here. They said there was too much screaming and hitting and out-of-control parenting.[3]

When I study violence in families and parent-child alienation, I think to myself, "If I could only convince parents to keep their mouths shut and their hands to themselves when they should keep their mouths shut and their hands to themselves, I would give to society a gift of inestimable value." Parents in distress should emulate Christ who, when He was brought as a lamb to the slaughter, "opened not his mouth" (Isa. 53:7). If parents would be Christlike when it is time to speak, peace would abide in their homes. In all of scripture, there is not a single reference to Christ raising his hand or voice in anger against a child.

Every modern-day depiction of Christ portrays a man of quiet dignity. In the sometimes chaotic universe of our homes where emotions scatter helter-skelter like leaves in the wind, I tell you, Mom and Dad, that with a quiet response bound by love, the wonder of God reveals itself. "God is the friend of silence," so said Mother Teresa (Spink, 19). Believe it.

I will end this chapter by quoting a wise but unknown author who penned a beautiful message to parents entitled "The Pause That Refreshes." It is a model of nonreviling parenting:

> I am the father of a large family. I go home tired from the routine of busy days. Before I cross the threshold I pause. I reflect for just a moment to remember what may be inside. Someone probably broke a dish. The carpet sweeper may be out of order. There may be a broken arm. The neighbor may be phoning us about a paper our boy did not deliver. There

---

[3] For those of you who would like to know all six complaints, I will list them here: (1) They were never sure what to expect or what was expected of them. (2) There were repeated inconsistencies in the application of consequences. (3) There were few or no meaningful consequences for inappropriate behavior: "I got away with too much." The consequences that were applied were virtually always aversive, mostly intended to cause pain and hurt, physically and emotionally. (4) There was so much screaming and hitting and out-of-control parenting. (5) There was too little tenderness (praise, touch, etc.) and too much harshness (criticism, fault-finding, arguing, etc). (6) There was very little laughter and smiling.

may be children to jump on me for attention and love (maybe with jam on their hands) to tell me the important happenings of the day.

So I pause and repeat a prayer something like this: "Oh, Lord, may my presence in this home bring faith and a cheerful good evening to those I love. May my homecoming strengthen this home and bring us together, not tear us apart. Keep my voice even, that I may build confidence and respect in me as their father and their friend."

This is the "pause that refreshes." I walk in prepared to act, happily and positively—not to react in an unbalanced way. It is amazing what it will do for me. We can try this not only in the home but also in a meeting that promises to be tense in which human relations are bristling.

The "pause that refreshes" is the priceless moment when we root the center of emotional gravity within us where it belongs, rather than in the social climate into which we are going.

What a great, Christlike message of nonreviling for parents. Remember, "grievous words stir up anger," but "a soft answer turneth away wrath."

Chapter Five

His Hand Is Stretched Out Still

Christlike parenting is parenting that never gives up. Despite the behavior of the children of Israel, who had "cast away the law of the Lord of hosts, and despised the word of the Holy One of Israel...his hand is stretched out still" (Isa. 5:24–25). I am particularly fond of the Lord's tender expression of commitment to His children found in Isaiah 49:15–16: "Can a woman forget her sucking child, that she should not have compassion on the son of her womb? yea, they may forget, yet will I not forget thee. Behold, I have graven thee upon the palms of my hands."

As a parent, it is clear that Christ would never turn away, tune out, or turn His back on His children. Though their behavior might be wretched, His "hand is stretched out still." There is an enduring message here for parents today: Like Christ, we must never give up on our children, no matter how badly they behave.

We must engraven them upon the palms of our hands, and those hands should be ever stretched out unto them.

Risks of Expelling Children From Home

As I sat with a group of fathers a few years ago, I was distressed by the direction taken in a discussion about what parents should do with their out-of-control teenage children. The general consensus was that if such children are unwilling to abide by the rules of the home, they should be kicked out. In support of this notion, one man recalled a situation with which he was personally familiar where a father kicked his unruly adolescent son out of the house. Because of it, "the kid learned the lesson he needed to learn and straightened up."

Hearing nothing that contested the notion that kicking the kid out was the right thing to do, and fearing that the discussion would end on that bitter note, I decided to speak up, I reminded those fathers that though I was happy the boy straightened up, the parents were mighty lucky! I then enumerated the risks of expelling ill-prepared adolescent children from the home and stressed why it is better, if at all possible, to keep such children home. I also emphasized the importance of parents learning the skills necessary to work effectively with such a child at home, as well as knowing how to work with other children in the home who might be adversely affected by such a son or daughter (as addressed in some detail later in this chapter).

Expelling unruly children from the home might bring a feeling of immediate relief to the parents and other children, but the long-range losses are far more likely to exceed any short-range relief. Children who are kicked out of the home are taught that their parents have no skills for dealing with unruly behavior, and they are left to wonder if their parents even love them. Being kicked out puts children in harm's way and makes them even more vulnerable to the damaging and even life-threatening dangers of drugs, ill health, disease, poverty, exploitation, and crime.

Being out of the home, they are completely beyond any positive family influences and almost totally under the influence of the very people and environments that have contributed to their already difficult circumstances. Set adrift, any small forward movement in their lives comes to a complete stop. Direction is lost; in fact, the child's life begins steadily slipping backwards. The breech between the child and a healthy peer group gets wider and wider. Before long such children are literally and figuratively wandering about aimlessly, but getting nowhere. While aimlessly out and about, they increasingly become a threat to their communities, engaging in mischief, mayhem, and crime.

A father once justified expelling his teenage son from home by citing Genesis 3:24: "So [God] drove out the man" from the Garden of Eden. As justification to drive a child out of the home, this doesn't cut it! Adam and Eve were adults. God was not being punitive. He was facilitating their growth, as is discussed later in this chapter when I talk about "learned helplessness." We must be careful that we don't distort scripture to justify our incompetence or cover our ignorance.

DO NOT KICK YOUR CHILDREN OUT OF YOUR HOME!

Keeping Kids at Home

Would Christ kick one of his children out? No! Like a good shepherd, He would go out to save the one that was lost (Matt. 18:11–14). That is Christlike parenting at its best. Christ reminded us that it is easy to love those who love in return: "[Do] not even the publicans so?" (Matt. 5:47). But to love those, to save those, to extend one's self for those who don't love in return...now that is being Christlike (Matt. 5:44–49). To the Romans, Paul declared, "Hath God cast away his people? God forbid" (Rom. 11:1). And God forbid that we should cast away ours, even if they "cast away" our love and entreaties, even if they curse us and despitefully use us, even if they "despise" our word. As does Christ, we must keep our hand stretched out still.

In the early part of 1997, I listened to a television rebroadcast of a sermon delivered by the Reverend Billy Graham. Speaking of Christ's enduring love, he said, "He has his arms opened wide to receive you." He further noted that "it was never God's intention for people to be lonely." These are powerful messages to parents of wayward children, most of whom are lonely for a loving family but are confused about how to be a part of one.

Nevertheless, the urge to expel unruly children from the home is often compelling. In the long run, though, there is a better way. We have found that when unruly children are kept home, under the influence of in-control, skillful parents, four distinct advantages are frequently realized:

1. *Children observe and experience proper parenting behaviors, and from this they learn the skills they will need to one day be good parents.* You can almost be certain that one day your children will be parents, and what a blessing it is to them and their children (your grandchildren) to have the skills they need to be good parents.

2. *While home, they are more likely to be in school acquiring the skills they need to succeed occupationally and socially as adults.* Most will graduate from high school, and though some might not, they are more likely to acquire marketable skills in trade schools, apprenticeship programs, and on-the-job training. Many will return later to earn their high school diplomas.

3. *Maturing at home is far, far better than simply getting older away from home.* As children mature, they begin to see things differently. If that maturing takes place at home, and they see and relate to already safe, mature adults, without even realizing it, they will gravitate toward those adults and begin to imitate the behaviors modeled by them. Several years ago, one of my sons lamented to his mother, "Mom, I'm doing exactly what I promised myself as a kid I'd never do. I'm behaving just like Dad."

Never forget this. When grown, children will typically emulate the behaviors of the adults they grew up with (Wahler and Dumas, 49–91). They will not continue to behave as they did when they were children. Paul the apostle taught us this valuable lesson nearly 2,000 years ago: "When I was a child, I spake as a child, I understood as a child, I thought as a child: but when I became a man, I put away childish things" (1 Cor. 13:11). The value of this lesson is immense as it relates to keeping our unruly children home within our sphere of influence, no matter how weak it may seem at times.

4. They will "connect" to the family. Though at the time they will seem totally indifferent, aloof, and even rude toward the family, in subtle ways they nevertheless identify with it. They will become "connected" (Resnick, et al., 823–32). They come to see the family as a part of them and themselves as a part of the family, as contrasted with being apart from the family. All this takes time, but it's time well spent. The time will pass, and it is far better to use that time to your and the child's advantage.

Many years ago when I was a young college student working on a home construction crew for my father-in-law, I was trying to encourage an able young co-worker to get a college education. He asked me how long it took to get through college. I said four to five years. He exclaimed, "I'd be 26 years old before I finished!" I asked him how old he'd be in five years if he didn't go to college. The point is clear: the same amount of time will pass doing things right as will pass doing things wrong, so you might as well do them right. Keeping children home within the structure of the family is, if at all possible, the right thing to do, even if it takes considerable time for the benefits of that to be observed.

All of these combine to dramatically increase the probability that unruly children will eventually succeed as self-sufficient adults, contributing members of society, and loving, valued members of the family. We must be slow to anger, patient, and long-suffering. One author encourages us to reject "the common assumption that present problems will last forever" and asserts that instead, "we must invest in children and teach them the perspective of patience—a simple but powerful belief that things will get better" (Hollar, 26). Shriver's and Allen's research reveals that under the right circumstance, noncompliance is a short-lived matter (173–76).

Consider the apostle Paul. He "breath[ed] out threatenings and slaughter against the disciples of [Christ]" (Acts 9:1). He "persecuted the church of God, and wasted it" (Gal. 1:13). He bound and delivered "into prisons both men and women" (Acts 22:4) and stood by, consenting to Stephen's death (Acts 22:20). In fact, he did "many things contrary to the name of Jesus of Nazareth," including imprisoning and approving the putting to death of "many of the saints" and punishing "them oft in every synagogue,...persecut[ing] them even unto strange cities" (Acts 26:9–12). Yet he became one of the greatest missionaries and disciples of Christ to ever live. In preparing to write this book, I did a brief study of the lives of people of our day who, though once "prodigal," have since become, in many ways, models. Here is a representative sample of what I found:

THEN:

Accused of murder and mayhem; his behavior in court was so disruptive that he had to be shackled and gagged; was later imprisoned.

NOW:

A volunteer for a major university community program encouraging youth to enroll in academic programs and to acquire functional life skills.

THEN:

A '60s rock star, heavily into drugs—to the point of passing out on stage during performances.

NOW:

A mainline entrepreneur who donates to charity all of the considerable profits of one of his enterprises. His charities include children's cancer research and treatment of seriously ill and traumatized children.

THEN:

A hard-core, disaffected, "nihilistic drug and alcohol addicted punk rock performer."

NOW:

Serving as a monk in a monastery where he is known as Father John. He is now dedicated to encouraging other disaffected youth "to open up to them the beauty of God's creation."

THEN:

A loved and nurtured teenager who turned his back on his distraught mother and father to pursue a rebel life in the fast lane of "drinking, drugs, smoking, girls, fast driving, and high-powered guns."

NOW:

A major force in a worldwide evangelical movement, a powerful preacher, and a committed witness for Christ.

There is hope!

Over the years, as I have worked with distressed parents of wild and ungovernable youth, I have been amazed at how many of these children grow up to become stable, happy adults with children of their own. A couple of years ago, a young mother was in my office concerned about the behavior of her three-year-old son. As she was about to leave, she told me that when she was a teenager her parents were about to kick her out of the house, but before doing it, they had come to see me. I advised them against it and discussed things they could do to keep her at home with the family.

It worked, and the girl told me how thankful she was. She had gone on to finish high school, which she wouldn't have done had she been forced to leave home. She acquired occupational skills thst made it possible to support herself as a young adult after she chose to move away from home. She was sure she would never have acquired those skills had she been kicked out of the house as a teenager. With maturity, she managed her life well, eventually marrying a fine young man who was a good husband and father.

What I told those parents, and what I tell many others struggling with similar problems, is what I am now going to tell you, in three parts.

1. Remain calm, composed, and direct.

When emotions are calm, parents are better able to express their concerns and expectations in a way acceptable to the child. It goes like this (for simplicity, I use the masculine pronouns):

Parent:	"Son, despite our differences, we would rather have you home than living somewhere else. How do you feel about living at home?"
Note:	Engage the child in the conversation as soon as possible; otherwise, he will assume that he's in for a lecture. He will shut down and will probably not hear a word you say.
Son:	"I don't know."
Note:	If he says "I don't know," respond with empathy and understanding, then come right back to your original question: "I can understand that this might seem a little awkward to you, but we'd like to know how you feel

about living at home." The probability is high that he will either answer the question or will give a reasonable approximation of an answer such as, "Hey, what's this all about? I live here because this is my home. This is where my stuff is. Where do you think I want to live, in the gutter?" Now we're getting somewhere. From such an answer, select out what is worth responding to and build on it, ignoring all the irrelevant verbiage (the "behavioral noise").

Parent: "Right. This is where your stuff is, it's where your family is, and even though we have some serious differences, it certainly beats living in the gutter. And by the way, we are glad you're a member of this family, differences or not."

Note: The boy will probably acknowledge what you said with a grunt or some other indifferent response. Just ignore that indifference. It's just "noise."

Parent: "As a member of the family, we have a few expectations that are common to everyone. For example, we expect everyone to be kind to one another. What else do we expect of everyone?"

Son: "Look, I know what you're getting at. You want me to go to church every Sunday, be a Goody Two-shoes, and all that crap. Well, I'm not going to and you can't make me. So if you want to kick me out, kick me out. I'll survive. It ain't like I got no place to go, you know."

Note: Be prepared for a defensive response. If there is anything the child doesn't want to do it's to tell the parent that he knows what's expected of him!

Parent: "You are right, Son. We can't make you behave one way or another, nor are we going to try. Your behavior is your business. We just want our home to be a safe, comfortable place for everyone. What can we all do to make it that way?"

Note: Again, use empathy and understanding, but come right back to your original question, though perhaps slightly varied.

Son:	"Oh, you want to know where your kids are every minute of the night and day. You want us to clean up after ourselves. You want us to do our chores. I know what you expect. What's this all about, anyway?"
Note:	Again, selectively attend only to those things you want emphasized. All the rest is just "noise." Ignore it!
Parent:	"You're right. We do want to know where you children are and for everyone to contribute to the general appearance and well-being of the home. Good response. Thanks. How do you relate to these expectations?"
Note:	Let the boy know that you appreciate his insight, even though it is shared with indifference and even disgust.
Son:	"Okay, Okay. I'll clean up after myself and do my chores, but beyond that, I'm not making any promises. You know how I hate your crummy rules, so don't expect me home until you see me."
Parent:	"We're happy for the assurance that you'll clean up after yourself and get your chores done. Regarding your whereabouts, that, too, is up to you. We just hope you'll take good care of yourself and use wisdom in the things you decide to do."
Son:	"Don't worry, I can take care of myself."
Note:	To the extent to which the child is unwilling to comply with family expectations, he deprives himself of privileges that would otherwise be available: the use of the car, allowance money, parental "taxi service," and so on. He needs to understand, of course, that these are not being taken away from him. Rather, he hasn't earned them, and he can only have what is earned. This is super important!

At this point, the parent would want to become specific about immediate concerns that threaten the sanctity of the home. These might include bringing into the home illegal drugs, pornographic materials, or badly behaving friends. These need to be addressed. The following three scenarios illustrate how this can be done noncoercively, using controlled substances as the object of concern.

Scenario #1:   Confronting the problem.

Parent:	"I understand you've been experimenting with drugs (or whatever). I can imagine that the pressures you experience to do that sort of thing must be pretty great. How do you feel about all of that?
Son:	"It's no big deal. We just mess around with it. No one's hooked. I'm not worried. Don't worry about it."
Parent:	"I appreciate the assurance that we have nothing to worry about, but, of course, we do. Why would we be concerned?"
Son:	"Parents are always worrying about something. I don't know why. Nothing that bad's going on. It's no big deal."
Parent:	"You're right. We do worry. Can you imagine why?"
Note:	The parent remained on course. Without being combative, the parent came right back to the question at hand: "Why are we concerned?"
Son:	"I guess it's because you think I'm going to screw up my life. Become a junk head. Get busted. Land up in the gutter or the slammer or the morgue. No way! I'm okay. I'm just having a little fun with my friends!"
Parent:	"You have a clear idea of where our concerns lie. You're right on target there! Thanks."

At this point the discussion could move in any one of several directions. The parent might continue to pursue concerns about the inherent dangers of "playing with fire." Should that course be taken, care must be exercised that emotions are kept under control, that a lot of advice isn't given, and the discussion doesn't go on so long that the child turns off.

The direction of the discussion could change to focus on things the child could do and skills that could be learned when, in time, the child decides he needs help and wants to change.

Don't be afraid to discuss with all the children a sibling's problems with drugs. The discussion could center on parental expectations and the natural and logical consequences of high-risk lifestyles. Should this be the direction the discussion goes, care should be taken to avoid ultimatums, coercion, guilt trips, or anything else that would further alienate the child from the family and its values.

Whatever direction the discussion goes, be certain you as a parent never allow yourself to be drawn off course onto dead-end paths. The discussion above might end with the parent saying simply, "Well, it's obvious we see this matter from very different perspectives. My appeal to you is to be very careful. We both know there are dangers inherent in these things. As your parent, I just don't want you to be hurt. You mean the world to me, so please, be careful. I love you." And let it go at that. The child will get the message. At the moment, that just might be the best you can hope for. The chances are good that opportunities will be available later to continue the discussion more productively. In the meantime, remember, today is not forever. Leave the door open for more talking. Your hand should be stretched out all the day long.

As the opportunity presents itself, it is important that parents kindly and unemotionally state their expectations to a wayward child, focusing on what the child should do rather than what the child should not do. Depending upon the disposition of the child, how to approach that would vary as illustrated by the following scenarios:

> Scenario #2:   The parents state their expectations to a misbehaving, though willing-to-cooperate, child.

Parent: "We are concerned that the other children might be wrongly influenced by the things you're doing. We need your help to make sure that doesn't happen. Will you cooperate with us?"

Son: "Sure. That's cool."

Parent: "First, though you have chosen to use tobacco/drugs/alcohol, you must never bring those things home, nor show them to your brothers and sisters. Can we count on you to comply with that expectation?"

Note: Get verbal agreement of each point along the way.

Son: "Yeah. Well, but what if I don't have any place to put them? What am I supposed to do, hide 'em in the shrubs?"

Parent: "When we say you are not to bring them home, we mean you are not to bring them onto our property or into the house. We don't have any suggestions for how you'll manage that. We only want to be sure they are never a part of our home environment. Furthermore, if we ever find any of those things on or in our property, they will be confiscated—no questions asked."

Note: The child must understand that how he solves his problems is his business and that you, as parents, will not facilitate in the least any use of controlled substances.

Son: "Does that mean you're going to search me and my room every day?"

Parent: "That's a fair question. Not regularly or without cause. However, if we have reason to suspect these substances are in the house, and are potentially dangerous to the children, we will look for them and confiscate anything we find. Why do we take this position?"

Son: "'Cause you don't want the kids to get started on the stuff. But if they do, don't blame me. I'm not the only one in their lives who uses this stuff, you know. You can pick this stuff up anywhere. That's how I got started."

Parent: "We're sadly aware of that. Furthermore, if we find drugs at home, we will call the police. Breaking the law at home is no more justified than breaking the law away from home. We will not allow ourselves to be made accessories to a crime. Why would we take such a strong position?"

Son: "Hey, I know what you're driving at. Don't worry. I'll keep the place clean."

Parent: "Good. We're glad you understand and are going to cooperate. One other thing. When talking to your brothers and sisters, never say anything to glorify the use of this stuff or to make them curious about it. Suppose one of the kids asks you about it. What will you say?"

Son:	"I'll just tell them to forget it. To bug off."
Parent:	"What would you say to discourage them from trying this stuff?"
Son:	"I'd tell 'em if they want to try, that's their business. But I won't encourage them."
Parent:	"We appreciate your help. Furthermore, we want you to be an active, participating member of the family. We want nothing to do with this stuff, but lots to do with you."
Note:	Don't get drawn into a discussion about the logic—or lack of it—behind what the child is doing with his life. That is "noise." Just be sure the child knows he is valued and is regarded as a valuable member of the family.

I realize that a discussion would not likely go just as I have portrayed it. The basic points to remember in any such discussion are (a) stay with your expectations; (b) be empathetic and understanding; (c) be clear about consequences; (d) avoid argument, reason, logic, good sense, appeals, threats, excessive or misdirected questioning, and anything else that will most certainly turn him off; and (e) assure the child he is valued and has your unconditional love. That's really the best you can do. If you try to force your position, the child can simply tell you to stick it in your ear and he'll be gone. You will be unsafe to be around and will have driven a wedge into the very space where you need to build bridges and bonds. Either way, it's risky, but building bridges and bonds between you and your children is a lot less risky than driving wedges between you!

Scenario #3:	The parents state their expectations to a misbehaving child who is less willing to cooperate.
Parent:	"We are concerned that the other children might be wrongly influenced by the things you're doing. We need your help to make sure that doesn't happen. Will you cooperate with us?"
Son:	"Hey, I got nothing to hide. This is me. I have nothing to apologize for or explain to anybody. I'm not hurting

	anyone—not even myself, despite what you think! I'm not the terrible person you think I am."
Note:	Again, stick only with your expectations. This is no time to get into a lifestyle or character analysis.
Parent:	"Will you cooperate with us in our efforts to make sure the other children are not exposed in our home to alcohol, tobacco, or drugs?"
Son:	"Whaddaya mean not exposed?"
Parent:	"We mean a couple of things. First, you must never bring any of this stuff onto our property or into the house, and secondly, you must never invite the children to use it or to become curious about using it. Do you have any questions at all about what we expect?"
Son:	"Hey, you can't tell me what to do with my stuff. If I keep it to myself you got no reason to worry. I'm not going to bother the kids. I want nothing to do with 'em anyway. The less I see of them the better."
Parent:	"We're pleased to know that you have no intentions of introducing the children to it. Thanks for that assurance. As far as what you do with the stuff, you need to know that if we ever find any of it at home, it will be confiscated immediately and reported to the police. No questions asked."
Son:	"Hey! Look! If I'm going to be searched every time I come home, or you're going to search my room when I'm not here, I just won't come home."
Parent:	"We have no plans to search you or your room unless we have reason to believe you are breaking the law and we could be accessories to the fact. We will not shield you from the law, nor facilitate your breaking it. Why would we take that position?"
Son:	"I know what you're saying. Okay. I'll try to stay clean at home, but I'm not making any promises."
Parent:	"Your efforts to stay clean at home are appreciated. Nevertheless, simply trying is not good enough. We expect absolute compliance. No exceptions. What do we mean by 'absolute compliance,' and 'no exceptions'?"

Son: "Look, I told you I'd do my best. Isn't that good enough? I'm not perfect you know. The most I can do is guarantee you that I'll try my best."

Parent: "We are glad to know that you will try. But if just trying isn't enough, you need to know that we will not shield you from the law—even at home. So what can you expect of us in such case?"

Son: "I guess it means you'll call the cops. Fine. Go ahead. I'll have to take my chances. That's the best I can offer."

Parent: "And we wish you well. Also, we really want you to be with us and to participate in family activities. We love you tons and enjoy having you around."

Note: Relative to both scenarios, the likelihood remains high that the child will bring "stuff" into the house. If illegal drugs are involved, you would be well advised to have the police (preferably in street clothes) search the premises. The child needs to know in advance that this is a distinct possibility. Home should be a refuge from social ills, not a safe harbor for social ills. When children learn that, they will soon come to value home, respect it, and hold it sacred.

If, however, the child decides that this is too constraining and elects to leave home, that's his choice. He is not a victim. He is an agent unto himself. Of his own accord, he will open that door, walk through it, and close it behind him. But knowing of his parents' love for him, he knows he can come back home through the same door. Furthermore, the likelihood of his coming back is very great once the child begins to experience the instructive consequences of his decision. It might go like this:

Son: "I'm going to get a place of my own. I can't stand living in this dump any longer!"

Note: Don't allow yourself to get into an argument over whether that's a good idea or a bad idea, whether home is or isn't a dump, or whether or not he can make it on his own. Rather, suggest something like this:

Parent: "We can understand your feeling that way. Being on our own is something we all want at one time or another. But before you leave, let's talk about some important things about living away from home. If you're going to strike out on your own, there are some things you need to know. We don't want you to get hurt."

Note: This puts the problem right back in his lap, while showing that you are concerned about his welfare. However, despite your well chosen words and empathy, he might not be in the mood to accept them; he might respond angrily by saying something like,

Son: "You don't care what happens to me. If you cared about me, you wouldn't make my life so miserable!"

Parent: (To which you would say, simply,) "I'm sorry you feel that way."

Then leave it at that. If the child insists that he is leaving, be prepared to talk very calmly as one adult to another about what it costs to live away from home. You might show him some of the bills you have to pay every month. I'm reminded of the time our oldest daughter decided she wanted to live in her own apartment. She was tired of being the oldest in the family of six children. She was working at a drive-in earning a salary that she thought she could certainly afford to live on. We sat down together one evening with paper, pencil, and a stack of bills and counted the cost of living away from home. After an hour of this adult exchange, she smiled understandingly, looked at me, and said, "I guess home isn't so bad after all." And that was the end of it. This gave me an opportunity to say, "I'm glad you decided to stay; we like having you around," and the whole matter ended on a high note.

Though angry, the child might want to think it over for a couple of days. This is fine. A couple of days of rational thinking about such an idea will almost certainly kill it, particularly if the child is given information about the cost of living away from home, since he will have to bear all those costs.

If the child decides to leave, let him leave. But remember, he leaves at his own expense! When he leaves, he must understand that he is making this decision at his own expense. This is not your decision, and, therefore, you have no responsibility to support it. I realize there are some risks involved here. We are talking about a risky time of life, but the odds are high that if the child leaves home at his own expense, he will be back within a couple of weeks and in a mood to work things out.

As the child leaves home, be emotionally upbeat. Let your countenance smile and shine upon him. Smile, give him a hug, say good-bye, tell him to drop by or call and let you know how things are going, since you are concerned about him. Ask him to leave you a telephone number so you can stay in touch in case something happens that he'd want to know about. Treat the situation the same way you would treat the occasion of other children leaving home to establish their own place in the world. Be upbeat, happy, and hopeful. This could be the child's first great opportunity to learn about independence. I realize we are living in a dangerous time, when drugs, sexual promiscuity, and sexually transmitted diseases are rampant. It is only natural for parents to worry that their children might fall victim to these dangers. But trying to force them to stay home is by no means a sure defense against their being exposed to or participating in them.

Working in your favor are the realities of living away from home. There is more to leaving home than just having enough money to support oneself. There is the loss of family companionship and of familiar surroundings. There is the loss of the conveniences of living at home: a readily accessible refrigerator and cupboards full of food, clothes washed and ironed and neatly put away in dressers and closets, the availability of a radio, a television, a computer, a stereo. All of these things are missed, and typically they are missed quickly.

Another thing parents have working for them in getting their children back home is the child's unfamiliarity with and lack of certainty about their away-from-home environment. Others in that new environment are not as predictable as members of the family. Moods are not the same. The child is less comfortable expressing his moods in that new environment. At home a child can explode and be out of sorts and still be loved. But as a guest in someone else's home or living with roommates, he can't get away with that kind of "junk" behavior. He feels less at ease about going to the refrigerator or into the cupboards for food, about arbitrarily changing the channel on the television or putting a tape in the stereo. A so-called "runaway" isn't in a new environment very long before he realizes just how much he has walked away from.

What parents typically experience is that the youngster will leave home (I prefer to call this "bolting" rather than running away) and be gone for a few days and not a word is heard. Of course, parents are anxious during these few days and envision all sorts of terrible things happening. Those visions are usually exaggerated. In a few days, the child will very likely call home. The call will generally be a pleasant one during which the child asks how things are going, how the dog is doing, what's new around the house, and so on. When this happens, be very pleasant and upbeat. Visit on the telephone pretty much as you would visit with another son or daughter who is "legitimately" on his/her own. Be sure to end the telephone conversation with a note of appreciation for the call and an invitation to drop by and visit anytime. Don't ask probing questions, and don't invite the child to move back home! He knows the door is open should he want to come back.

Shortly after this telephone conversation, the child will very likely drop by the house and survey the kingdom that he abandoned a few days earlier; typically this will increase the desire to be back home. This sort of posturing will continue for only a few days, often resulting in hints on the child's part that he'd like to come back home. As a parent, you would want to assure the child that would be fine, but don't fall all over yourself with enthusiasm. Keep it all very even and calm.

With the child back home, a good opportunity exists to sit down and calmly discuss the problems that led to the departure in the first place. Negotiations are easier. It also gives you a chance to reiterate the value system of the home and the expectations to be met by those who live there. With teenagers, particularly older ones, negotiations are fine so long as they don't rob the child of his moral agency, destroy the value system of the home, or undermine the parents' position of leadership. Such negotiations should be calm, pleasant, free of ultimatums, and void of any hint of parental smugness: "Well, we knew it wouldn't last long. We just hope you learned your lesson." Regarding control versus moral agency, it is so important that parents not try to force compliance. Denying a child the opportunity to exercise his moral agency is every bit as bad as what the child might do when exercising his agency.

I repeat, the longer you can keep your children at home during their adolescent years the better! Do not throw your children away! Do not encourage them to leave. In the long run, everyone is much better off if you are willing to put up with some of the stress, strain, "noise", and junk behavior that goes with growing up. Even a few additional years at home will give you time to bond to your children and give them time to learn necessary survival skills. Whether they stay or leave, there is going to be some pain and discomfort, maybe even misery and agony. But generally, in the long run, everyone is better off if the family can be kept together while children are in their formative adolescent years.

In my years of working with families whose teenagers have threatened to run away or leave home, and who have left home, in every instance where the parents took a reasonable, proactive position such as the one described here, their children were back home within a couple of weeks, things at home became better because of it, and in the end the situation worked out pretty well. But in those instances where children are kicked out of their homes or leave home unprepared to support themselves adequately, the lives of everyone—parents and children—are miserable. There is a price to be paid in child rearing. We either pay it for a little while up front or for a long while after adolescence.

I am absolutely convinced, all things considered, that up to young adulthood, the vast majority of children would rather live at home than away from home. Sure, there will be bad days when they'll want to be gone and you'd like to have them gone! But those days pass quickly. One of the tenderest moments of our parenting years came when our oldest daughter was seven years old. It was a summer Saturday, and Louise and I were working in the yard. Karen wanted something she couldn't have and went off in a huff. After about an hour, we realized we hadn't seen her for a while, so I went into the house to see what she was up to. There was no Karen, but on the kitchen counter was this note:

> Dear Mommy and Daddy.
> I have ran away. I am at Vickie's. Call me
> when you feel to cry.
> Karen

Though she was angry with us, she knew we loved her enough to cry about her absence. Remember, you should keep your children at home and as much a part of the family unit as possible, even though their presence might at times be distasteful. In this regard, talking with the other children about the errant child's behavior is a good thing. When doing this, be careful that attention is drawn to the character of the behavior, not the character of the child. Love and concern for the child must stand above all else! The behavior is what is not good. Be sure the other children in the family feel free to talk about the problem without it turning into a lecture about "And for heaven's sake don't you do those stupid things!" This brings us to a crucial, point:

2. Turn a troubling circumstance into a positive learning experience.

It is important that the other children in the family understand your position relative to their wayward sibling(s). Properly handled, this can be a great learning experience for them and an opportunity to explore with them the worth of every family member and of the family value system.

The following scenario illustrates how this can be done. Certainly, every family needing this help will require a different twist on the actual words used, but the basic message is the same: "We love our brother. We want to do all we can to help him. He is doing things of his own choice he shouldn't be doing, and he is paying a bitter price for it. By behaving as we should, we are ultimately better off." If the conversation makes those points, the probabilities are great that everyone in the family will grow and that blessings will emerge out of a tragic circumstance.

Scenario #4:   The parents visit with the other children about the behavior of a misbehaving sibling.

Parents:	"We want to visit with you tonight about Peter. We have some serious concerns. April, why do you suppose we are concerned?"
Note:	Get the others into the conversation as quickly as possible.
April:	"I guess it's because Peter is doing things that are wrong."
Parents:	"Yes. Unhappily for all of us, Peter has decided to do some things that can be destructive to a person. Things that can ruin a person's life. When we say 'ruin a person's life,' what does that mean, Joseph?"
Joseph:	"Well, I guess it means it can hurt them in some way. Maybe even kill them."
Parents:	"Exactly. And because of that, we are seriously concerned about Peter. We would never want something like that to happen to any of our children. Not Peter, not you, not anyone."
Greg:	"Ah, it isn't that bad. You're making it sound a lot worse than it is. Peter's just messing around. It's not that big a deal."
Parents:	"I hope you're right, Greg. At the moment, that's our biggest hope. But what Peter is doing is very, very risky. What do I mean, Greg, when I say 'very, very risky,' and why would that concern us?"
Greg:	"It means that Peter is taking some big chances with his life and could get hurt. And you don't want that to happen. But I still think you're blowing this out of proportion."
Note:	Notice how the parent is not arguing with Greg about the seriousness of the situation. That's a beside-the-point matter and should be ignored. Stay with the central issues: Peter is behaving badly, is in harm's way, and could get badly hurt. How badly is beside the point.
Parents:	"Thanks for hitting the nail on the head regarding our concerns. Peter is taking big chances and certainly could get hurt.

"Nevertheless, despite the fact that he is behaving badly, we love Peter as much as we love any of you. All of us must be kind, say nice things, be complimentary whenever we can, be playful and fun, and do nothing that would suggest we are angry or disappointed. Mary, what is something you can do when Peter comes home that will show you love him?"

Mary: "I can give him a big hug and a kiss and say I love you."

Parents: "That would be wonderful. I'll look forward to seeing you do that."

Greg: "That's all fine, but what bugs me is when Peter gets away with stuff we can't do. I have to be in by 10:00 P.M. on school nights and midnight on weekends. Peter comes home whenever he darn well pleases. That's just not fair!"

Parents: "You've raised a very important point, Greg. It doesn't seem fair. But Peter pays a price for coming and going as he wants. What is that price, Greg?"

Greg: "Well, he never gets to use the car, for one thing. And he doesn't get an allowance. I guess that's it."

Parents: "That's part of the price he pays, certainly. Would it be worth it to you, Greg, or any of you children, to pay such a price to behave that way? What about you, April? Would you be willing to give up all telephone privileges, your allowance, and any new clothes, to name a few, for the privilege of coming home late at night?"

April: "No way!"

Parents: "What about you, Joseph? What privileges would you be willing to give up just so you could come home after hours?"

Joseph: "I guess you're talking about my Nintendo, my bike, my allowance—that kind of stuff. I'd rather come home on time."

Parents: "I think you guys have gotten the point. Peter isn't getting anything for free. He is giving up a lot of things that none of you want to give up. Peter is paying a very big price to behave the way he is behaving.

"Greg, a moment ago you raised the issue of fairness. This really isn't a fairness issue. It's a matter of how much one is willing to give up to behave in a certain way. When you get to be Peter's age, you will be able to do the things you want to do, despite how we or anyone else feels about it. We hope you will make wise decisions that won't cost you or hurt you. What do we mean when we say 'decisions that won't cost you or hurt you?'"

Greg:	"Oh, I suppose you mean giving up things like the use of the car and stuff like that."
Parents:	"That could be part of the cost. What else? What if the decision is to break the law? What can that cost you?"
Greg:	"If it's bad enough, it could cost me money or even my freedom."
Parent:	"How else might that hurt you?"
Greg:	"Well, a police record can ruin a person's reputation— sometimes for life!"
Parents:	"Precisely. And what a terrible price that would be to pay. "April, what would the cost be to you if you resisted the temptation to take drugs? If you said 'NO' and just walked away? How costly would that be?"
April:	"Oh, it might cost me a friend. Then again, maybe it wouldn't. Maybe there wouldn't be any cost at all, only benefits."
Parents:	"What do you mean, no cost at all, only benefits?"
April:	"Well, a real friend would never offer me drugs, and by staying clean, I have good health."
Note:	The parents steered the discussion away from negatives and toward positives. They got the children thinking about how much better off they are, in both the long and short run, by behaving well.

Children can benefit greatly by learning early in life to delay gratification. A hallmark of intelligence and maturity is the ability to put off until the right time—the correct time—reinforcers which if gotten too soon can interfere with long-term gains:

—dropping out of school to take a job that pays what, at the time, seems like a big wage, only to be deprived of the skills needed to ultimately prosper financially;

—engaging in premarital sexual intimacy because of its immediate gratification only to be left with a troubled conscience, the real possibility of an unwanted pregnancy with its overwhelming responsibilities, the loss of youth, and even a deadly disease; and

—drug, alcohol, and tobacco abuse, which brings an immediate though false sense of acceptance, belonging, and with-it-ness, only to be left with life and health in ruins.

As we study the lives of high- and low-risk individuals, virtually without exception, how well they are doing in life and how happy they are can be accounted for by their ability to delay immediate gratification in preference to those things that are in their best interest:

— schooling and skill acquisition first, then long-term employment;
— saving first, then spending;
— marriage first, then sexual intimacy;
— healthy lifestyle followed by a healthy life;
— and so on.

Opportunities to teach this important lesson to the other children in our home are often made available by the lives of family members who do not delay gratification or reinforcement and are suffering from that. It's a way of making lemonade out of a lemon.

Remember, behavior is shaped better by positive than by negative consequences; by being positive and "solution oriented" rather than negative and "problem oriented," probability for growth in the right directions increases.

A recent study demonstrated that in homes where children and their parents are able to talk with one another free of the risks of criticism, lecturing, judging, moralizing, etc., the probability of children experimenting with drugs in the first place is half that of children who come from homes where parents and their children have problems talking with one another (Miller).

3. Lovingly apply earned consequences.

Parents typically hate to see their children suffer, even if that suffering is self-imposed or earned. But to rob children of the lessons to be learned from their own behavior is to rob them of a great blessing. As the Lord had promised, Adam and Eve suffered death because of their transgression (Gen. 2:16–17; 5:5). After warning Adam and Eve of the consequences for eating the forbidden fruit, the Lord allowed the consequences of their choice to teach them important lessons. When Adam and Eve partook of the forbidden fruit, God didn't say, "I've decided to give you another chance. Death seems kind of harsh for eating a piece of fruit."

But parents do this all the time. They state their expectations, enumerate the consequences, then protect their children from the natural consequences of their bad choices. That's a terrible thing to do to children. Children need to understand that behavior generates consequences.

"Natural" consequences are forces for sustained growth and improvement in the lives of our children. Some lessons can only be learned from natural consequences. If a child behaves carelessly and gets hurt, he or she should certainly find comfort from a compassionate, understanding parent. But learning to avoid being hurt in the future is learned best by the pain and discomfort caused by the carelessness. At such times, parental compassion and understanding should not—I repeat, SHOULD NOT—get in the way of the lessons to be learned from the natural consequences of a child's ill-advised use of agency. To do so is to allow mercy to rob justice, and tragedy is sure to follow.

Though mercy never really robs justice, parents frequently attempt to use mercy in a way that robs their children of valuable lessons that can be learned in no other way. They literally rob their children by taking away from them something they have earned and that rightfully belongs to them: Consequences! Such robbery is a moral crime. Though Christ's hand is stretched out still, we must not assume that it spares the disobedient the natural consequences of their behavior (Isa. 5:25).

For some time, I worked with the mother of a drug-addicted son. He was nearly 30 years old. For all intents and purposes, he was well beyond her sphere of influence. Still, she held out hope for him, as all such parents should. Unfortunately, as she stretched her hand out still, it always had money in it, and it always got bitten.

Her son rarely came home, but when he did, he was disheveled, sick, and broke. He would plead for help: "Mom, I have no money. I need your help! I love you. You are my only hope."

He assured her, "This time I am getting my act together. I've learned my lesson, Mom. I promise. Please believe me. Please trust me!" as he looked at her through pleading eyes.

The mother cried. The boy cried. They cried together. They embraced. It was all so tender and touching (as he prepared to put the "touch" on her). They held hands and visited. It was like old times. They had a bite to eat, and across the table they talked and smiled. Hope for a better tomorrow gushed forth, eclipsing reality. (Remember: past behavior is the best predictor of future behavior.)

The stage was repeatedly set for a double crime. He callously robbed her of her meager retirement reserves, and she tenderly, "mercifully" robbed him of the lessons he could only learn through natural consequences: the lessons he had to learn if there were to be any real hope at all for his recovery—a hope that grew ever dimmer with each tender, "merciful," selfless gesture.

Parents in similar situations typically ask me, "But what do I say? This is my child. What do I say?"

Following is a scenario which illustrates my answer:

Son:	"Mom, I have no money. I need your help! I love you. You are my only hope."
Mother:	"I can see that you are in desperate circumstances. My heart goes out to you."
Note:	Mother did not assume any role as her son's problem solver by asking what she could do to help. Past experience had taught her that he didn't want her help, he

wanted her money. Nor did she become caustic by saying, "I can see you are in desperate circumstances—of your own making, I might add!" or "My heart goes out to you, but not my money!"

Son: "Mom, I need some money, bad! I need help now! This will be the last time I ever bug you about this. I'm getting it together, Mom. Really!"

Mother: "I'm glad to hear that you're getting it together, Son. That's a step in the right direction for sure."

Note: Notice how Mom put all the wailing on extinction and carefully selected out for her attention the only thing worth attending to: "getting it together," even though he really wasn't!

Son: "Mom, I know you have a tough time believing me. We've been through this before, and I haven't been honest with you. But believe me, this time's for real. I just need some temporary help and I'll be fine. Just this one last time, Mom. Please."

Mother: "I sure hope you *are* on the road to recovery. I'm sorry you're experiencing these problems, but I'm glad you know the way out of them."

Note: Heartrending confessions of guilt were no assurance of repentance. Mom stuck by her guns. She wasn't hoodwinked into believing that reality is shaped by words alone.

Son: "I only need a couple of hundred dollars, Mom. Will you please loan me a couple hundred dollars? I'll pay you back in a few weeks. You can depend on it."

Mother: "Son, you've convinced me that you need help, but since money is not the answer, I will neither loan nor give you any."

Son: "Mom, please. It's different this time. Really different. Just a loan of a couple hundred dollars."

Mother: "Sorry, Son. No more money."

Note: Nothing was said about her needing the money for retirement, etc. That was beside the point. He hadn't the slightest interest in how secure she was in retirement!

Son:	"I can't believe this, Mom. Here I am on the verge of recovery, and you refuse to help. I thought you loved me more than that."
Note:	Guilt trip time. Proceed with caution.
Mother:	"I wish you well with your recovery, but don't drag my love for you into this conversation. That's beside the point."
Note:	It's time to set the record straight on some important things, one of which has to do with what love is or isn't. One thing it isn't is the key to Mom's bank account!
Son:	"What you're telling me, Mother, is you don't really love me. You love your money, but not me. Thanks a lot! I'm out of here. Don't be surprised if you never see me again. In fact, don't be surprised at what might happen to me. And don't think I didn't try to get my life together, thanks to no help from you!" He storms out in a huff.
Note:	And who knows? Maybe he would have gone out and done some extra stupid thing and suffered badly because of it. But that would not be Mom's doing nor her responsibility. It was purely and simply the natural consequence of a child's deliberate decision to violate the commandments.

As sad as that was, Mom did the right thing. She did not impose suffering on her son. Neither was it her wish that he suffer. This was not an act of vengeance. Remember, vengeance belongs to the Lord (Deut. 32:35). Furthermore, this boy is back. This quote from a letter from his sister and brother-in-law was heartwarming: "This took many, many months, even years of consistent work. We had to be firm and empathetic. This all proved extremely successful. He began reading religious materials and scriptures. He began to see where he had been and where he wanted to be. He actually asked for help and not money. He admitted to his abuse and lying and was sorry for what he had done, and asked for help in overcoming his addictions and behaviors. This was a complete turnaround." They went on to note that, since he was so "behaviorally fragile," that to help him avoid "resorting to his old ways," they set "small and attainable goals on the road to bigger goals." It worked!

Letting a child experience natural consequences is especially important whenever a child violates the law. Whether in or out of the house, he *must* experience the consequences of his choices.

When a Child Threatens Violence

While living at home, a volatile teenager might harbor a lot of anger and occasionally turn to threats of physical violence. He might threaten to hit others in the family with the intent of hurting them or threaten to damage property. Of course, this simply cannot be tolerated! This is a risky situation and might be too complex for easy resolution, but if it does occur, and there is a possibility the child really will be violent, let the child know that if he elects to behave in a violent way, you will need to call the police and you will press charges.

Assault and battery are no more excusable at home than on the streets. If a child can't be physically restrained and threatens to hurt someone through physical assault, particularly if there is some notion that the behavior might actually occur, parents should call the police to intervene. Children should know that it is not an idle threat!

If you have to defend yourself physically, do so short of striking back. Do not get into a physical exchange of blows, even if you are altogether able to do so. To strike back does nothing but encourage the child to lash out even more viciously and with more determination. If possible, leave the house and make your way to a safer environment from which to seek help. Let the child know that you are not going to respond in kind. He might be out of control and behaving in a very stupid way, but you are in control and behaving rationally.

Again, the Savior provides the perfect model for how to behave in such a situation. Accosted by his persecutors, the Savior could have called down "more than twelve legions of angels" to retaliate in His behalf (Matt. 26:53). But to have done so would not only have been reactive, it would have negated the sacrifice Christ was going to make on the cross. To do so would have been disastrous. That is the message you need to clearly understand. Striking back is potentially disastrous. Still, the message you need to deliver to the child is that violent, irrational behavior carries with it severe consequences.

I'm reminded of a situation where a family feared that a 17-year-old son would sometime become violent and could be dangerous. We role-played how they would respond if that occurred. Shortly thereafter, the parents' worst fears were realized one night when the boy came home angry and was about to physically take it out on his parents. The father, as we had role-played, gently raised his hand as a signal to the boy to stop and said in an authoritative, bold, though controlled voice (no shouting):

"Stop! (Pausing for two to three seconds while making eye-to-eye contact.) It's obvious you are very upset. I'm sorry your evening hasn't gone well. *Before you hit anyone* you need to know how we will respond if you do. We will call the police and we will press charges! You will spend time in the juvenile detention center, and you will suffer the full consequences of the law. Furthermore, you will lose every privilege this home has to offer, including the use of the car, the telephone, and so on! (Followed by another three second pause.) Now, before you hit anyone or do anything for which you'll be sorry, go to your room and think it over. We will be here when you return."

The parents then stood there, calmly looking the boy straight in the eye. Silence fell over the room. The boy realized that he was not intimidating his parents in the least. They had a plan to deal with his inappropriate behavior. They were in control. He had no plan for dealing with the consequences of his behavior. He was out of control. Everyone just stood there looking at each other. The parents were firm and composed. The boy was angry and trembling. After what seemed to be a long time—but was only a few seconds—it became obvious to the parents that the boy had run out of steam and was not going to follow through with his threats. The father, in gentle tones, said, "I'm sorry you've had such a bad day, Son. I'm sorry you're upset. Go to your room now and regain your composure. Then let's talk about it in the morning."

He walked over to his son, put his arms around him, gave him a hug, a kiss on the cheek, and told him that he loved him. The mother did the same. The boy went to his room and that was the end of any subsequent threats of physical violence.

The key to preparing for such a problem is to predict what might happen (based on past experiences), prepare a response, then practice that response. Remember, your response must find you in complete control, must demonstrate to the child that you are not about to be intimidated, and should the child behave violently, clearly understood earned consequences will be borne immediately by the child.

Do not try to talk through the child's problem, hostilities, and anxieties until after the child is calm and in control. The time to talk about problems is when the child is able to talk about them rationally and calmly. Never try to resolve a problem when a child is drunk, stoned, angry, or enraged.

Regression

When working to recover wayward children, time becomes a particularly important consideration. We have learned in the study and treatment of human behavior that (1) even under the best of circumstances, behavior once improved has the tendency to regress (that is, return back) toward the way it was before treatment; (2) lasting change occurs incrementally (that is, little by little rather than all at once); and (3) even with the best treatment known, some behaviors might never improve, in which event we endure. The ability to endure adversity well is surely a Christlike trait. Consider what Christ had to endure, as recorded in the 27th chapter of Matthew. Christ was scourged, spit on, flogged, insulted, then crucified. And what was His response to this? He beseeched His Father to forgive His persecutors for they knew not what they were doing (Luke 23:34).

Think about it in the context of parenting. It is the same with our children. In a figurative sense, we sometimes get trampled on through verbal abuse, exploitation, and disrespect. Nevertheless, like Christ, we must extend to such children our loving kindness and our long-suffering. That is how Christ would do it. That is how He did it.

Parental suffering is often aggravated when a child's progress is interrupted and even regresses. Parents must realize that as the behavior of their once wayward child improves, the threat of regression (i.e., going back to the old behavior) is constantly lurking in the shadows. We must not lose faith and falter. In the storm at sea, when Peter saw Christ walking on the water, he called out, "Lord,...bid me come unto thee on the water." Christ answered, "Come." But as Peter walked toward Christ on the water "and saw the wind boisterous, he was afraid" and began to sink (Matt. 14:28–30). He lost faith. He regressed. But he called again upon the Lord for help, "and immediately Jesus *stretched forth his hand* and caught him" (vv. 30–31; emphasis added).

I observe the regression effect work on parents who, after having made remarkable improvements in their ability to parent non-coercively, go back to their old punitive, coercive ways. They regress when the winds are "boisterous" around them. A recent letter from a mother said it well: "My biggest challenge now isn't knowing what to do, it is always doing what I know I can and should do."

This is such a compelling problem in parenting that I am going to take a moment now to highlight what is found in scripture about the regression effect. I do this for emphasis—and I do it in the hope that you will be continually mindful of it and will guard yourself against it:

Matthew 13:21–22 "Yet hath he not a root in himself, but dureth for a while: for when tribulation or persecution ariseth,...by and by he is offended...and he becometh unfruitful." The lesson for parents here is to take root by learning and using effective parenting skills.

John 21:3 With Christ gone, Peter said to his associates, "I go a fishing. They say unto him, We also go with thee." Momentarily, their ministry ended and they returned to their old trade.

Galatians 1:6 "I marvel that ye are so soon removed from him into that called you into the grace of Christ unto another gospel."

Galatians 4:9, 11 "After ye have known God,...how turn ye again to the weak and beggarly elements, whereunto ye desire again to be in bondage...I am afraid...lest I have bestowed upon you labour in vain."

Hebrews 2:1 "Therefore we ought to give the more earnest heed to the things which we have heard, lest at any time we should let them slip."

2 Peter 2:22 "But it is happened unto them according to the true proverb, The dog is turned to his own vomit again; and the sow that was washed to her wallowing in the mire.

To minimize the probability of regression, there are at least three conditions about which parents should be careful:

1. *As emphasized earlier, allow consequences to deliver the intended message. Interfering with that message reinforces inappropriate, maladaptive behavior and encourages children to regress.*

Our responsibility as parents of wayward, misbehaving children is to help them, as best we can, to improve the way they behave. Getting even is not the intent. My dear friend and colleague Dr. Carl Cheney, professor of psychology at Utah State University, put it nicely when he reported, "Simply making someone's life less pleasant without appropriate behavior change seems obviously an unacceptable approach."

Parents must be clear on this important point. Suffering for misdeeds has value only to the degree to which it leads to improved behavior. If our children's suffering is a natural consequence of behaving badly, our prayers and hopes should be that such suffering will be instructional. There should be no delight at a child's suffering because "he got what was coming to him." Furthermore, we should rid ourselves of the nonsensical notion that suffering should involve pain, that without physical pain as a punisher, the necessary changes in behavior will not be effected. This is totally without support in either science or scripture. I recall an article in our local newspaper about a teacher in Florida who "punished" misbehaving students by kissing them with "bright red lipstick." Hardly "painful" physically, but still punishing.

Remember, let consequences deliver the message. There are no lessons as exquisite as those taught by the consequences of our own behavior.

2. Maintain an in-control demeanor.

Even though you might feel terrible inside about the child's slippage, at least appear to be up and "with it." Let the child know by your demeanor (i.e., your countenance) that though he might be slipping, his parents are not. Lord Mountbatten put it nicely: "If you want to be a leader, you can't go about like a shrinking violet. You may have to put on a bit of an act. It must be sincere; it's not good to have a bogus act. You've got to play up any qualities you have and blow them up larger than life." There is a great message to parents in this leadership advice. Be careful what your demeanor says.

3. Never tell or warn a child he is slipping back to his old ways. He already knows it!

Never tell a child something he already knows. Rather, increase your positive acknowledgments of his appropriate behavior. Progress is two steps forward and one step back. Acknowledge the forward steps and ignore the backward ones.

Here a little and there a little, that's okay. Behavior that develops, changes, and improves in small, incremental steps is more likely to last and is less likely to regress. Small and simple things can effect great gains (2 Kgs. 5:13–14).

When working to recover our wayward children, we must resist the temptation to try to quickly effect gains that are too great. Whether it's losing weight or regaining a child, patience, long-suffering, and small, incremental gains produce the most lasting results.

My studies of families in crisis have revealed that if, while children are wayward, their parents remain strong; are a model of mature behavior; maintain a happy, loving relationship with their children; and project a Christlike countenance that shines upon them, when the children grow out of adolescence, the probabilities are high that they will gradually, incrementally return to the family and its values. In fact, about 95 percent of such children "come back" if the parents remain high on the scale of maturity, thus providing the standard to which the children will ultimately gravitate.

In Proverbs 22:6 we are taught to "train up a child in the way he should go: and when he is old, he will not depart from it." In my work with families, I have found this to be true. *When he is old, he will not depart from it.* But when he is young, well, that's a different matter. Youth depart from "the way" all the time. But when these youth become adults—that is, "old"—if well taught and nurtured, they are far less likely to remain apart from those teachings, particularly if their first teachers, their parents, taught them as Christ would have them taught. The widowed mother of a large family made this cogent observation: "My children are not all active in church, but they are all good kids, and one day they will come back."

The Road Back

The road back is an uneven one. My research has revealed that wayward children return to the family value system in stages. They tend to return first to the social and economic values and ethics of the family. This is precisely what we would expect, knowing what we do about human behavior, which tends to move in the direction of things that are most *immediately* reinforcing. Being socially skillful and adroit wins friends and the attention of family and co-workers, so it is immediately reinforcing; hence, as did Paul the apostle, they "put away childish things," such as bizarre, thoughtless, socially immature behavior.

Early in their return, children tend to emulate the family values of work, economics, and self-sufficiency. This, too, is to be expected, since success in these areas brings immediate reinforcement in the form of money which can then be exchanged for desirable goods and services.

A return to the spiritual dimension of the family value system is typically longer and slower in coming because the reinforcers for behaving in a spiritually appropriate way are less immediate. It isn't until marriage, children, and the realities of the limits of mortality (including trauma) come on the scene that the reinforcing effects of spiritual things begin to have an effect on behavior.

It is in times like this—and this is a very important point for parents to seriously consider—that the behavior of the parents is even more important than the behavior of the wayward child. I am certain that Christ expects more of parents than He does of children during times of recovery. When you think about it, that only makes sense. Of particular importance is that parents remain buoyant, optimistic, and Christlike—that they keep their countenance up!

Though most errant children, once they become adults, will return to the family in some degree, some children will resist any and all attempts at repatriation. For their parents, the frequently given advice of the Lord to endure is sufficient (1 Pet. 2:19). No one will drag their children kicking and screaming into heaven. For such resistant children, only in time, and perhaps not until eternity, will the matter be resolved.

When dealing with human behavior, predicting the effects of treatment can be made only in terms of probabilities, not certainties. As with medicine, we can never be absolutely sure the selected treatment will give us the relief we want when we want it. Nevertheless, every effort is made by the therapist and the doctor to heighten the probabilities that the desired results will be realized. And so it is with human behavior. We do our best, then patiently and lovingly wait.

Adult Children

A question frequently raised, especially by parents of "adult" children, is "What is a child?" Obviously, there is no simple answer to this question, but there are some guidelines that can help answer the question. For example, if a child is in college (or trade school or an apprenticeship program) and living at home while steadily and seriously pursuing an education, it is not unreasonable that the resources of the home (i.e., food and lodging) be made available to the "child" in support of progress toward ends that will eventually lead to independence. Still, the child should be doing all he or she can be reasonably expected to do in support of those ends. Children can earn wages. They can pay training and/or education-related expenses such as tuition and books, and they can contribute to the general well-being of the home, and so on.

My experience working with families with older children has suggested that under such circumstances, remaining at home is reasonable until the "child" is 25 to 26 years old. By about the age of 26, we have essentially come to the end of our physiological growth (Bijou, Personal communication). Beyond that age, in nearly every instance, it is in the child's best interest to be on his or her own, learning the skills needed to survive and prosper independently.

On a case-by-case and temporary basis, it is appropriate to provide a reasonable level of support at home for an older "child" who is experiencing unforeseen trauma: job loss, divorce, illness, disability.

Problems arise when adult children (usually 20 years old or older) who are able to be independent choose to remain at home while making no reasonable contribution to their support and while making no move in the direction of independent living. They pay no rent or utilities. They contribute only marginally if at all to the purchase of groceries. They are often unemployed or underemployed, and they compromise the general quality of the home environment by behaving badly. In a word, they are "sponging" off their parents.

Not infrequently they increase this burden to their parents with their own children to whom the parents, now grandparents, become the primary caregivers. This "boomerang kid" phenomenon is becoming a growing problem, one for which parents must be prepared to take sometimes uncomfortable steps.

In instances where older children (18 years old and above), for all intents and purposes, are "squatters," they are being done no favors by being allowed to remain at home in a state of dependency. As noted by Dr. Martin Seligman, when people "learn that reinforcement and behavior are not contingent on each other," they acquire "learned helplessness" (551–53). What this means, simply, is that if people are in a situation where there is "motivational deficit," that is, there is no reason to do anything to improve their circumstances because no matter how they behave the reinforcers supporting helplessness continue to flow, they will do little to change. In fact, they will be as exploitive as possible. Furthermore, their behavior is often made more distasteful by a lot of complaining, immaturity, low levels of productivity, and the like.

To support such "children"—to contribute to their learned helplessness—is tantamount to allowing mercy to rob justice. I have found that the years between 18 and 26 are remarkably important years during which children learn the skills of independent living. Every year lost during that time to "learned helplessness" is a year lost from the important business of learning to be self-sufficient.

I am reminded of research done on the behavior of poultry and reptiles whose emergence from their shells is "helped" by someone cracking their shells open and letting the animals out, sparing them all the hard work of pecking their way out. Invariably, the long-term effects of this "help" on the behavior of those animals is negative, including lower survival rates, difficulties in thriving, and a host of other problems. Similarly, in our zeal to help our children, we can run the risk of hurting them in the long run. They are typically better off when they are given opportunities to "peck their way out of their shells." I realize that taking steps to rectify such situations carries with it serious risks, particularly where grandchildren are involved. Each case needs to be treated separately and might require professional, including legal, help. But the effort is generally worth it.

For some "children" such an effort might be the only thing that wakes them up to reality. Once on their own, they might very well falter, stumble, and even fall. That's okay. In the process of recovering, they will have learned some valuable survival skills. Striking out on one's own for the first time is generally an uncertain matter, even under the best conditions. It isn't unusual for kids to come home from time to time to check things out, to make certain "their" room is as it was and is ready for reoccupancy should the need arise, and to raid the cupboard of a few canned goods. It can take a little while before they get up to full power.

During the Vietnam War days, I was doing quite a lot of work on the island of Guam. On the north end of the island is Anderson Air Force Base from which B52s, heavily loaded with bombs, took off on bombing missions to Vietnam. The end of the runway was the end of the island, dropping several hundred feet nearly straight down into the sea. Many pilots and crew members told me of the sinking feeling (literally and figuratively) they often felt as their planes left the runway and began dropping toward the ocean, being so heavily loaded. But before long, with sufficient power, they would recover, gain altitude, and be on their way.

That is a good analogy to what is frequently experienced by children who strike out on their own. Though there might be an initial sinking feeling, our children usually learn what they need to know and get the power they need to go aloft, to be on their way independently. But these lessons can only be learned by personal experience, and the longer kids stay home beyond the age and time they should be on their own, the more helplessness they learn.

Christ, though being the Son of God, was made perfect through what He learned, some of which caused Him to suffer (Heb. 5:8). There is a lesson there for us mortal parents as we nudge our children from the nest.

But in instances where the unruly child is just that, a child—typically early 18 years old and younger—my position remains unchanged: If at all possible, keep the child home and connected.

As parents, it is our responsibility to do all we can, within reason, to preserve our children, then to keep our hand stretched out still so that they can return to the family and its values. But only time will tell, so endure it well and emulate Christ. The biblical account of the selling of Joseph by his jealous brothers serves as a good reminder that when we do the will of the Lord, His hand will be there to preserve us.

After Jacob's death, Joseph's brothers were worried that Joseph would hate them and take revenge (Gen. 50:15). Instead, Joseph forgave them, erased their fears, and reminded them that "God meant it unto good,...to save much people alive" (v. 20).

Today is not forever. We must patiently look beyond the moment and take the hand of God to lead us away from fear and despair unto good. There is a great parenting message in that. Give it some thought.

Chapter Six

THE GARMENT OF PRAISE FOR THE SPIRIT OF HEAVINESS

It is inevitable. Our children will do foolish things, just as we did, do, and will continue to do. After all, we, too, are children. No matter how well they are taught and nurtured, as children come under the influence of unhealthy environments, their behavior will yield to some extent to the influence of those environments. It is predictable. Nevertheless, most youth nurtured in a loving family make it into adulthood intact, positioned to make a valuable contribution to society, despite the foibles of human nature that at one time or to some degree might have led them "into divers temptations." To increase the probability of their children's success, parents need to learn the value of building up, and building on, their children's strengths.

The prophet Isaiah supported this principle when he proclaimed that the "Spirit of the Lord God" had anointed him "to give unto them beauty for ashes, the oil of joy for mourning, the garment of praise for the spirit of heaviness; that *they might be called trees of righteousness*, the planting of the Lord" (Isa. 61:1, 3; emphasis added).

I recently wrote a paper for educators on the difference between punishment and discipline. In the paper, I make a distinction between "discipline" as a means of teaching and punishment as a means of simply administering pain. "Discipline" means "training that corrects"; therefore, a child's misbehavior should be "disciplined" in a manner that trains the child to behave correctly. "Punishment," on the other hand, means to "inflict suffering, pain, or loss that serves as retribution." Well, you tell me, which is the Christlike approach?

Reinforcing Positive Behavior

Dr. Sidney W. Bijou, one of the world's greatest behavior scientists, has taught us that the most effective way to teach children to behave well is to strengthen desirable behavior through positive, reinforcing means, and that the least effective way to reduce problem behavior in children is through the use of aversive or negative processes (*Behaviorism: History and Educational Implications*, 444–51). In other words, if you want your children to behave well, pay attention to them when they are behaving well. A simple "Thank you for picking up your toys" or "That was kind of you to help your little brother" or "You sure seem to be enjoying that book" is sufficient. When acknowledging such behavior, be brief. The fewer words you use (I suggest no more than 12), and the less time it takes to say it (five seconds or less), the better.

Unfortunately, just the opposite is what we observe in most families, particularly in high-risk families; that is, families where there is a high incidence of problem behaviors. In my observations within family settings and my work with parents, I have been troubled to find that parents typically ignore 95 to 97 percent of all the appropriate and good things their children do. But if a child misbehaves, parents are five to six times more likely to pay attention to that misbehavior—and virtually always in a negative, aversive, coercive way. As one mother put it in a letter to me, "America is diseased with threatening, spanking, and using other coercive measures in an attempt to control children." Since parental attention is the most powerful consequence in the shaping of children's behavior, guess which behaviors are most likely to get strengthened?

Attending to inappropriate behavior in punitive, coercive, reviling ways is to build a family on a foundation of sand, and when the "rains" descend, the "floods" come, and the "winds" blow and "beat" upon that home, it falls, and great is the fall thereof (Matt. 7:25–27).

A basic lesson parents must learn early in their child-rearing years is that a child's disinclination to behave "well" is a signal that parents are *not* acknowledging and building on the child's strengths. There is a better way than scolding to turn weaknesses into strengths. For example, suppose that a child uses profanity. Definitely a "weakness." Rather than simply trying to punish and scold profanity out of the child, the parent should *teach clean speech* and make it more reinforcing than profane speech. That's making weak things become strong. Remember, children do not learn how to behave from punishment because it is not instructive. They only learn how *not* to behave. Christ would teach his children how to turn weakness into strength.

The following scenario illustrates how that might be done in the case of a child using profanity:

Parent: "We've noticed, Son, that every day during the last two weeks you have been using swear words. This is simply not acceptable. Why is using profanity such an inappropriate thing to do?"

Note: The parent didn't ask the child to explain why he swore. *Do not ask children to explain their inappropriate behavior.* It is better to ask a child why a behavior is not appropriate since that invites the child to become part of the problem-solving process, a part of the solution.

Son: "I don't know. Everybody at school does it. I didn't think it was such a big deal."

Parent: "Just because others do it does not mean it is right or good. Think of one reason why you should not swear."

Note: The parent did not allow the child to sidetrack the moment by getting into a discussion about the rightness or wrongness of swearing. The parent stayed on course and simply repeated the question.

Son: "Well, I guess it's wrong to swear. That's what you've always told me."

Parent: "Others may not believe it's wrong, but we do, and we are happy you know that. And besides, it just doesn't sound good. It makes people think you don't know a better way of expressing yourself. What are some words you can use other than swear words to express yourself?"

Note: The child has been briefly reminded about a characteristic of the family value system. An occasional reminder to this effect is good. The child is then invited to further explore a solution.

Son: "I guess I could say *darn* and *heck* instead of those other words."

Parent: "Good answer, Son. Those words are better than swear words. There isn't a single swear word that can't be replaced by a better word. Can you think of anything else you can do other than use swear words?"

Note: You will notice that every time the parent has spoken, it took only a few seconds to say what was said and ask what was asked. In this last instance, it would take less than 15 seconds for the parent to say all that was said. It is important for parents to keep the child actively engaged in the discussion. *If children think they are in for a long lecture, they will tune a parent out immediately.* They might be looking at the parent and even have a facial expression that suggests they are listening, but their minds can be a million miles away. The best remedy for this is for parents to *speak for short periods of time using only a few words* and then *invite the child into the conversation.*

Son: "Ah, gee, Mom and Dad. This is embarrassing. I know what you're telling me, and I'll try really hard not to swear around the house anymore."

Parent: "You're right, Son, swearing can cause embarrassment, and we are happy you feel that way. We are also happy you have decided not to swear around the house. But we expect you to stop swearing everywhere. What do we mean when we say we want you to stop swearing everywhere?"

Note: The parent has selectively reinforced an appropriate response, then expanded on it: "We are happy you have decided not to swear around the house. But we expect you to stop swearing everywhere."

Son: "Oh, I guess you mean when I'm at school and when I'm with my friends and wherever I am. But that's going to be hard to do! They all swear, and I'm going to look weird if I don't swear with them."

Parent: "We can understand you may feel uneasy at first, but we still expect you to control yourself and to use better language. To use the words you suggested would be good substitutes for swear words. You know what we expect, and that's great. We will just have to trust you to do that when you are away from home. Can we trust you, Son?"

Note: The burden of responsibility for cleaning up his language still rests where it should—with the child. The parents have acknowledged they can't control his behavior when he is away from home, but *they still expect him to behave appropriately*. Furthermore, *they have committed him to respect their expectations.*

Son: "Well, I'll try, but it's going to be tough."

Parent: "Thank you for giving us that assurance, Son. Maybe at the end of each day you can write in a notebook about how successful you were in using better language. And in the morning before you leave the house for school as you go out the door, say to yourself, 'Today I will control my language.' Will you do that?"

Note: Self-monitoring and self-prompting are forms of self-management and are well-established strategies for helping us improve our behavior. They work as well for children as they do for adults.

Son: "Yeah, I can do that. Is that all you wanted to talk to me about?"

Note: Children will often use comments like this that *cue* parents *it's time to stop.* If the parents feel their point has been adequately made, well understood, and well responded to, then it is probably time to stop. Stopping before you are entirely through is not always bad. Remember, today is not forever. This is not the last time you will ever have an opportunity to discuss your expectations with your child. It's better to leave a situation with the door open for further discussions. If, however, you feel that the child might lose self-control from time-to-time, a discussion of consequences would be in order.

Parent: "We are almost done, Son. We need to talk for a minute about what you can expect when you do or don't use swear words around the house. When you control yourself and only use good words, you'll be able to continue to enjoy many privileges that you really like around here."

Note: This would be followed by a brief discussion of what those privileges are: TV, his bike, and so on. It would be well to have the child tell you what those privileges are. Once this discussion has been completed, proceed with the discussion of consequences.

Parent: "And if you lose control of yourself, Son, what privileges will you deny yourself?"

Note: Then follow this up with a discussion of the privileges the child will deny himself and for how long they will not be available. (For a more detailed discussion of how to identify and apply consequences, see Chapter 5, "A Word about Consequences," in Latham, *The Power of Positive Parenting.*)

Doesn't this sound better than exploding and reacting in-kind?

Focusing on Weakness

Too often parents assume that when a child misbehaves, "what that kid needs is a good lickin'!" If you ever feel that way, I hope you'll reassess the situation and conclude that what that child needs is a good *lesson* in how to behave properly, and you're just the person who knows how to teach it. When you do that, give yourself a pat on the back, a hearty smile, some affectionate verbal praise, and maybe even a gold star on your forehead!

As just one example of Christ's position relative to children, consider this (Matt. 18:2–10):

> And Jesus called a little child unto him, and set him in the midst of them,
>
> And said, Verily I say unto you, Except ye be...as little children, ye shall not enter into the kingdom of heaven.
>
> Whosoever therefore shall humble himself as this little child, the same is the greatest in the kingdom of heaven.
>
> And whoso shall receive one such little child in my name receiveth me.
>
> But whoso shall offend one of these little ones...it were better for him that a millstone were hanged about his neck, and that he were drowned in the depth of the sea....
>
> Take heed that ye despise not one of these little ones.

Yet, how often we hear children described as being "full of the devil." How often we hear frustrated parents say, "I'm going to beat the devil out of that kid." While writing this chapter, I read an Associated Press article in our local newspaper which reported the indictment of a mother in New York for the murder of her six-year-old daughter "because she believed the child was possessed by Satan."

"Beating the devil out" of people has a long and ugly history, dating back centuries. The "Roman laws of chastisement" (circa 750 B.C.) sanctioned wife beating and even murder for certain domestic infractions (Myers, 496). The Crusaders of the eleventh, twelfth, and thirteenth centuries, and the Inquisition of the fifteenth century, inflicted hideous cruelties (revilings) on non-Christians in an attempt to cleanse them by "beating the devil out of them." The Salem witch trials of early Colonial America were attempts to force the devil out of men and women accused of sorcery and possession of "malignant, supernatural powers" (Guiley, 87–89, 291–300, 369). Giles Corey, as a case in point, was accused of being possessed of the devil and suffered a uniquely horrible death. Rather than being burned, flogged, drowned, or hanged (the most common methods used to drive the devil out), he was crushed to death beneath rocks, as recalled in the ballad "Giles Corey":

> "Giles Corey," sayeth the Magistrate,
> "We'll press it out of thee."

We look back in disgust on those benighted attempts to cleanse the earth of sin, not realizing that dark shadows of that past are very much with us today. Punishment focuses entirely on weaknesses and does absolutely nothing to build on or to encourage strength. It is an approach to discipline built on the notion that if weaknesses are beaten out of a child, strengths will be able to emerge and fill the space once occupied by those weaknesses. This is nonsense!

As parents, this means we must carefully measure our actions, our words, and even the tone of our voice. In the third chapter of James is found some wonderful advise for parents: "Even so the tongue is a little member...that...defileth the whole body,...an unruly evil, full of deadly poison" (vv. 5–8). "Out of the same mouth preceedeth blessing and cursing. My brethren, these things ought not so to be" (v. 10).

Parents, control that "little member" of your body. Speak softly to your children. Not only does it turn away wrath, but your kids will be more likely to listen to you. Shouting and speaking loudly are *not* characteristic of good child rearing; rather, it has been found that there is a strong correlation between how loud people speak and their degree of self-control. The louder they speak, the less self-control they retain. This is nothing new. As Christ stood before the angry masses, they "cried out..., Crucify him!" (Mark 15:8, 13). At Stephen's stoning, the mob "cried out with a loud voice" (Acts 7:57).

Christ's behavior was in stark contrast to His detractors'. He was quiet, serene, and in control. His enemies were loud, wroth, devious, scheming, and out of control. In the midst of their shouts and cries, he went "as a sheep to the slaughter...[and] opened not his mouth" (Acts 8:32). Parents, give some thought to that as a model for your verbal behavior. Remember, "Pleasant words are as an honeycomb sweet to the soul, and health to the bones" (Prov. 16:24).

Given all that is now known about human behavior, I am absolutely astounded that ignorance and Dark-Age systems for fixing behavior persist today. And they do persist. With regularity we read and hear reports in the media about society's desperate attempts to manage behavior by striking, shaking, and squeezing those who misbehave. Swatting kids is analogous to drowning our sorrows with alcohol. There might be a moment of short-term relief, but that is sure to be followed by long-term burdens of dramatically increased proportions. You can count on it! It's called countercoercion, and it is predictable! Short-term compliance achieved through coercion leads only to worse behavior in the long run.

Inflicting physical punishment is an absolutely skill-less approach to problem solving. Remember, it takes absolutely no skill to inflict pain on others, and inflicting pain is exactly what we do when we parent without skills. It's a large, worldwide human problem. Two researchers in Brazil found, relative to the families they studied, that "most parents believe that education meant to spank and that respect was obtained with the whip" (Coura and Rocha, 5).

As noted by Larry Brendtro and Nicholas Long, "The history of child-rearing in Western civilization is deeply rooted in the belief that we can 'scare the devil' out of children" ("Rethinking Respect," 2). It is my impression, given the troubled families I've worked with, that 90 percent of parents attempt to get rid of children's weaknesses by using punitive, coercive forms of discipline: hitting, spanking, squeezing, shouting, threatening, and so on. I have been amused at the popular soap ad that encourages consumers to "shout it out," meaning to use a particular brand of soap to get dirt out of clothes, much like we try to get "dirt" out of kids.

As I observe the behavior of those who attempt to beat or shout the devil out children, I see an old flaw: the strong acting out their anger and frustrations and ignorance on the weak. A crying inconsolable baby or a misbehaving child is so vulnerable.

I'm sure the picture is clear to you. An adult seething from a bad experience, one who can't strike back at the source of his or her anger, lashes out at a helpless or an out-of-sorts child. The child is an easy and handy target. The adult even provides self-justification: "You little brat! Shut up! I'll show you what you can expect when you behave that way!" Then, WHAM! All, of course, in the child's best interest. Not uncommonly, the name of Deity is profanely drug into the mess in a weak attempt to dignify it: Then the carnage begins.

Christ did not teach us to beat one another. He taught us to love one another. All nine beatitudes advise us of the blessings that come from doing good things (Matt. 5:3–11). Concerning the woman taken in adultery, Christ did not condone stoning her. In fact, he never even mentioned the word *adultery*. Rather, he said, "Neither do I condemn thee." Then to turn a weakness into a strength, he was instructive—not punitive. He said, "go, and sin no more" (John 8:11). The lesson in this for parents is overwhelming in importance: focus on what the child should do rather than on what the child should not do.

Building on Strengths

We must turn our attention to strengths and give as little attention as possible to weaknesses. Recalling Dr. Bijou's wise counsel, "The most effective way to teach children to behave well is to strengthen desirable behavior through positive, reinforcing means. The least effective way to reduce problem behavior is through the use of aversive or negative processes" (*Behaviorism*, 444–51). There is no better way than to build on your child's strengths!

In my many years of working with parents, I have yet to be asked, "What should I do when my children behave well?" Yet that is the most important question of all. That is the question that focuses on strengths. That, I am sure, is how Christ would parent.

After I'd spoken to a large group of women in Southern California on "The Power of Positive Parenting" (i.e., parenting which builds on strengths), a mother with anguish written all over her face cornered me about her 16-year-old son. The father had abandoned the family, was paying no alimony or child support, and she and her four children were hurting financially. "My son just won't get a job!" she exclaimed. "We need the money he could earn. What can I do to make him get a job?"

After discussing the boy and her options, I made a number of specific suggestions. She chose several she felt would work. As she was about to leave, I said, "Tell me more about your son. What kind of a boy is he?" Her eyes lit up, she smiled, and she launched into a proud mother's description of her son: "He's a very good boy. He gets good grades in school, has wonderful friends, is an Eagle Scout, is active in his church activities, and is good to his brother and sisters." By now she was beaming with pride. Then I said, "I am surprised you never mentioned any of those good things to me, that you seemed only concerned about his problems." "Well," she said, "that's what has to be fixed. Why talk about things that don't have to be fixed?"

I experience this repeatedly, week in and week out: "Our daughter is a good girl and we love her, but..." and from that point, everything focuses on problems. As I point out repeatedly in this book, problem-oriented thinking is not an effective approach to child rearing. Solution-oriented thinking is.

In an article entitled "Fixing Flaws or Building Strengths," the terms "chest-beating" and "flaw-fixing" are used to describe "treatment philosophies...that have been in vogue since the mid-twentieth century,...[treatment philosophies that] have been preoccupied with deficit and deviance." The authors note that "placing deficits in the foreground blinds [us] to strengths and potentials" (Brendtro and Ness, "Fixing Flaws," 2). The authors make a compelling case for "cultivating strengths" which focus on "providing the supports and skills that permit youth to meet needs and surmount life's difficulties" (4).

This is what parents must do. The following scenario illustrates how that can be done in a situation that could easily get mired down in a preoccupation with weaknesses and shortcomings.

Parent:	"David, this report you wrote for English is really good! I had no idea you wrote so well and thought so deeply!"
David:	"Aw, it's no good and you know it. You're always saying stuff like that just to make me feel good."

Typically a parent will respond with a statement to refute what the child has said. For example:

Parent:	"No, David, I didn't say that just to make you feel good. You really do write well. I mean it! This is good work!"

Armed with the ammunition provided by such a response, David fires back, arguing in defense of his own shortcomings!

David:	"Look, I'm stupid and you know it. It really makes me mad when you say things about me you know aren't true."

And the battle is on! Allowed to take its course, I've seen this kind of situation get progressively worse with every exchange until it ends up something like this:

Parent:	"Okay, David, okay. So you're stupid and no good! Have it your way. I was only trying to help. I only wanted you to feel good about yourself, but if you can't accept that, then that's up to you. I don't care to discuss this anymore. So much for my good intentions! How do you think this must make me feel as your parent!?"

Even with our best intentions, if we are not careful, it is easy for an attempt to build a child up to get off course. As a society, we are so problem oriented that we tend to gravitate in that direction. If we are not careful, we are goners.

Let's revisit the situation with David and illustrate a better way. We'll start from the beginning:

Parent:	"David, this report you wrote for English is really good! I had no idea you wrote so well and thought so deeply!"

David: "Aw, it's no good and you know it. You're always saying stuff like that just to make me feel good."

Parent: "I'm sorry you feel that way, but I'm not a phony, and you do write well. You don't have to believe me if you don't want to, but I'd appreciate it if you did. After all, I wouldn't want you to think I'd lie just to make you feel good."

Now what can David say? With this response, David's ability to write is a given. The issues on the table now are the parent's genuineness and David's choice to believe the parent or not. Let's consider what David might say and how the parent might respond so the channels of communication are kept open and, over time, the parents can continue to be strength oriented.

David: "I didn't say you were a liar. I said you just say those things to make me feel good."

Parent: "But that's lying if I don't mean it, and I do mean it. And you wouldn't want me to be a liar. I love you, David. You're a neat guy. What do you say we have a game of Ping-Pong?"

A response like this completely defuses David's argument that he is no good, that his parents are simply sheltering him from his own worthlessness. Furthermore, it provides an avenue for the boy and his parent to have a positive relationship, which will certainly open up other opportunities for the parent to build on the boy's strengths:

Parent: "David, you play a mean game of Ping-Pong. You might have beaten me this time, but next time, watch out. I'll take you on again tomorrow night."

David: "You're on, Dad. You'd better be tough."

I've used the example of Ping-Pong. It could be checkers or chess, *Trivial Pursuit*, marbles, or any number of things. It makes no difference so long as the experience is a positive one and the door is left open for a continuation of positive experiences. But be sure to pick activities in which the child is able to compete and even win. Don't invite the child to an activity that invites more failure into his life!

Let's suppose, however, that David's response is hostile, and argumentative.

David:	"Aw, it's no good and you know it. You're always saying stuff like that just to make me feel good."
Parent:	"But that's lying if I don't mean it, and I do mean it. And you wouldn't want me to be a liar. I love you, David. You're a neat guy.
David:	"Don't give me that junk! Everyone knows I'm a failure, and I can't stand it when people say stuff like that!"
Parent:	(Completely changing the subject) "I heard that the high school baseball team has won five games in a row. Not bad!"
David:	"What's that got to do with this conversation?"
Parent:	"Nothing. I just don't want to argue. Let's play a game of Ping-Pong."

Either way, the parent did not allow the conversation to degenerate into an argument over the parent's motives or into a fruitless attempt to convince the child he is able and does have worth. And best of all, the door to the future was left open, a future in which other opportunities could be created to build on the boy's strengths.

Building on strengths requires patience and time. People, no matter what their ages, don't get strong simply by having their strengths identified one time. It is a little-by-little process. A memorable experience of several years ago with a young man I'll call Ned nicely illustrates this important point.

Ned's parents are among the finest people I have ever known. They had raised a wonderful family and were active, contributing members of their church and community. Despite all of the good things that characterized their lives, they had become over-whelmed with Ned's behavior. He no longer participated in church activities, he had taken up with friends whose influence was of great concern to the parents, and he seemed to be moving further and further away from the values held so dear by his parents.

The parents had "done everything to talk some sense into Ned's head." Predictably, those efforts only made things worse, and in desperation the parents called me to see if there was something I could do to "bring the boy to his senses."

Though the boy had a lot going for him, all they could see were his so-called weaknesses. Their immediate concern was the boy's plans to spend the summer "bumming around Europe with his friends." The task given to me by the parents was twofold: first, to "talk some sense into the boy's head," and second, to talk the boy out of wasting his whole summer and all his year's savings "bumming around Europe." I agreed to see the boy, but made no promises as to how I would deal with the situation.

At the appointed time Ned showed up. If I live to be a thousand years old, I will never forget the look on his face nor his countenance as he entered my office. It was altogether evident that there were at least ten thousand other places Ned would rather have been at that time. Indeed, his countenance had fallen. Nevertheless, out of deference to his parents, he kept the appointment.

After giving him a hearty handshake and offering him a seat, with a broad smile on my face and enthusiasm in my voice, I said, "Your folks tell me you're planning to spend the summer touring Europe. Is that true?" He nodded his head in the affirmative and grunted out something that I interpreted to mean "Yes" as he waited for me to detail the folly of such a decision.

To his utter amazement, I responded by telling him how wonderful I thought it would be to have an opportunity like that and how as a young man I had wished that I could have done the same thing. He was surely in for an experience that could enrich the rest of his life! (I emphasized the word *enrich*.)

I can vividly recall the smile that creased his face. He began to sit up a little straighter in his chair. He sustained eye-to-eye contact with me, and the expression on his face suggested that he was inviting me to say more. So I did. I told him how important I thought it is to fill our youth with happy memories and to enrich our lives with wholesome adventure and excitement. I then asked him to tell me where he was going and what he was hoping to see and do.

That was all the prompting he needed. For the better part of an hour, Ned excitedly regaled me with vivid descriptions of happy times to come. Though he had reluctantly met his obligation to his parents to visit with me, he was not giving me any signs that he was anxious to leave. I wanted the visit to end on a substantive note, so I asked him to do me a favor. He answered simply, "Sure."

The strategy I used employs what is known in behavioral therapy as "behavioral momentum." If the therapist can get behavior (verbal or otherwise) moving in the desired direction, with lots of agreements and positives, the probabilities increase greatly that any reasonable suggestion by the therapist will be received agreeably. By now there had been a lot of positive interactions which, cumulatively, heightened the probability that a subsequent encounter would be agreeable.

I said, "While you're touring Europe, promise me that you'll do three things. First, write a postcard to your parents every week just so they will know where you are and that you are well. Tell them what a great time you're having and that you love them. Second, if you should ever have problems seek help from a reliable source such as your church, the Red Cross, or the Salvation Army. Third, you are creating memories that will last a lifetime. Create only those memories that will enrich your life. Create only memories you will be happy about and will want to share with your children and grandchildren. Will you do those three things?" He answered simply, "Sure, I can do that." This was the strength I had elected to build on: his willingness to cooperate with a simple request.

As Ned got up to leave my office, he stood tall, his chin up, his back straight. With a big smile on his face, he enthusiastically shook my hand. Our parting was in sharp contrast to our meeting just an hour earlier, and I wondered as he turned away what would become of him.

The years passed quickly. I took a position with another university hundreds of miles away, and we totally lost contact with Ned and his family. With all I had to do in assuming a new position, I didn't give much thought to Ned.

One day, out of the blue, came a wedding announcement and an invitation to attend Ned's wedding reception in a community about 20 miles from where we lived. I suddenly found myself bathed with curiosity over what had happened during the intervening years. My wife and I were excited as we approached the building where the reception was being held. Being unfamiliar with the building, we went in the wrong door, entering the reception hall on the opposite end from where the reception line had formed, but directly across the hall from the bride and groom. Almost immediately his eyes met ours. Instantly he bolted from the reception line and ran across the hall to greet us. His face was alive! His eyes glistened, and a smile etched his face from ear to ear. He was a tall boy, and learning over he took me into his arms, gave me a big bear hug, and quietly said, "Dr. Latham, it saved my life." That's all he said, but we both knew what he was talking about.

We later learned that after his "bumming around Europe," he entered college, where he met his bride and eventually graduated. He subsequently took a position in city government in a community not far from where we lived. This young man and his lovely wife are the parents of several children, are active in their church, and are stalwarts in their community. That day of parental despair over 20 years earlier was not forever. Forever, as it turned out, got brighter and brighter by the day.

This experience illustrates another important benefit derived from focusing and building on strengths. We have learned that if behavior improves in one area as a result of noncoercive treatment, it will likely improve in other areas without treatment. The experience of one of my fine students illustrates this nicely (Reed, 367–68).

Curt was concerned that his six-year-old daughter was whining too often, so he discussed the matter with one of his professors. Curt took data for a week (called baseline data) to find out how often his daughter whined and also to find out how he was interacting with her when she whined and when she didn't. He took data each day for a week between 4:00 P.M. and 8:00 P.M. This is what he found:

Average number of times his daughter whined: 13

Average number of times he was negative/coercive (meaning he tried to stop the whining, typically by scolding his daughter): 10

Average number of times he was positive (focused on strengths): 3

As you can see, the negative interactions outnumbered the positive ones by a ratio of just over 3 to 1. (We urge parents *never* to have more than one negative interaction to every eight positive interactions.) With a ratio of three negatives to only one positive, it was no wonder the problem behavior occurred so frequently. That was the behavior getting all the attention! Something had to change, and it did.

Treatment had two parts. First, Curt decided to just completely ignore the whining behavior. This meant that when his daughter whined, he would just turn and walk away or in some manner put the whining entirely "on extinction." Second, from time to time while his daughter wasn't whining, he would pay attention to her. You will recognize this as the "selective reinforcement" of non-whining behavior. The father's attention was turned to strengths rather than weaknesses—solutions rather than problems.

The effect of this treatment on his daughter's whining was dramatic. After seven weeks, the whining behavior was completely gone. Also (and this is very important to note) by the eighth week, Curt was averaging 20 positive interactions per day and no negative or coercive interactions. (Now that's more like it!)

But perhaps most dramatic of all was how, by focusing attention only on strengths, the child's behavior improved in other areas. In his report, Curt noted: "My daughter's appropriate behavior generalized to several other behaviors without any formal intervention including:

1. Getting out of bed in the morning without being told.

2. Making her bed daily.

3. Getting ready for the day without the usual help from Mom or Dad by

      a. dressing herself

b. combing her hair

c. putting her stuffed animals on her bed.

4. Setting the table for breakfast.

5. Following her parents' model by hugging and reinforcing her brothers, sisters, and parents.

6. Being generally helpful with family/home activities.

They built on strengths. Even though there were heavy demands on their time, they found the time and the means to build their children up as Christ would do, rather than tearing them down as Satan would do.

My data reveal that in healthy families, that is, families in which children are happy with their parents and parents are happy with their children, parents have no more than one negative interaction with their children for every eight positive interactions. Drs. Betty Hart and Todd Risley, reporting the results of their monumental study of verbal behavior in families, found that in healthy families, parents were six times more likely to say positive, encouraging, supporting things to their children than negative, critical, and prohibitive things. Such parents "gave their children affirmative feedback every other minute, more than 30 times per hour" (126). Hart and Risley found that the effects of "enriched language" in stable families and "impoverished language" in unstable families produced lifelong "intractable" disparities in children (16).

Giving Praise

Parents must be positive and build on their children's strengths. There is simply no better way of creating emotionally, behaviorally, and spiritually healthy children. NO better way!

Proper use of verbal praise is one *very* effective way of giving children affirmative feedback. Not only is this taught to us by good science, it is taught to us by good Christianity. Paul admonishes us to think about whatsoever things are honest, just, pure, lovely, or of good report, virtuous, and *praiseworthy* (Phil. 4:8). Shouldn't we especially look for these things in our children, compliment our children for them, and let our minds dwell on them? Paul said he could "do all things through Christ which strengtheneth [him]"

(Phil. 4:13). Shouldn't we seek to strengthen our children as Christ strengthened Paul? The Psalmist tells us "praise is comely for the upright" (Ps. 33:1; 147:1).

There is a powerful message in this for parents. Since these are the behaviors valued by Christ, they are the behaviors that should be valued by us, and when we observe them in our children, it follows naturally that we should acknowledge them in some appropriate way.

There are many ways we can give praise. Among the synonyms for *praise* are: *approval, congratulations, acceptance, acknowledgment, appreciation, approbation, blessing, to cheer or cite, commend, compliment, to esteem or honor, laud, recognize, recommend, salute, sanction, thanks, tout,* and *give tribute,* etc.

Among all these possibilities aren't there one or two you could use with each of your children? I have suggested earlier that parents make a list of the appropriate things their children do and keep that list handy as a reminder to acknowledge those behaviors.

The positive acknowledgment of appropriate, praiseworthy behavior remains among the most powerful means of shaping and maintaining healthy behavior in our children. The appropriate use of verbal praise should meet the following conditions:

1. Praise must be deserved. Undeserved praise is hollow and unconvincing. Children can spot it a mile off—and it turns them off. For example, a parent says to a child who has grudgingly done one nice thing for the first time in his life: "Oh, Billy, you are *always* such a good helper."

2. Praise must be given sincerely. It's possible to do this whether you want to or not. If it is deserved, it should be recognized. Revisiting Billy from the earlier example, the parent wants to see that only-once-before appropriate behavior reoccur. Simply, sincerely saying "Thanks Billy. I appreciate that" will raise the probability that the behavior will, indeed, reoccur.

3. Praise should be given casually and briefly. As I noted earlier, it is typically not necessary to use more than a dozen words or to take more than five seconds to say them. My observations reveal that if parents talk more than seven seconds, children quit listening.

4. Praise should be delivered intermittently. That means randomly, *not* continually. Constant praise for every good thing done turns kids off. The intermittent schedule of reinforcement is the most powerful schedule of reinforcement. It is an intermittent schedule of reinforcement that keeps the economy of Nevada so robust. (Las Vegas is one of the fastest growing cities in America!) Think about it! (Remember that praise is only *one* way to give children positive, encouraging, or supportive feedback, and other forms can and *should* be used often.)

5. Praise should occasionally and fittingly go beyond the acknowledgment of compliance to the level of values. I spoke earlier of this. Billy does a good job on his homework:

"Billy, not only are you a good student, you're a boy who sees a job through to completion. Super!" (Though more than 12 words, it takes only five seconds to say.)

Of the good works of others, Paul said, "They have refreshed my spirit and yours: therefore acknowledge ye them" (1 Cor. 16:18). What a sweet thing for Paul to say, and what a sweet, Christlike message for us today, nearly 2,000 years later. When our children do things that refresh our spirits, "acknowledge ye them."

Chapter Seven

Choose You This Day

A Christian Model

One of the greatest lessons God taught in the Garden of Eden was a lesson on choices and consequences. Let's review that lesson as it applies to our role as parents. Carefully consider the instruction given to Adam by the Lord: "Of every tree of the garden thou mayest freely eat: But of the tree of knowledge of good and evil, thou shalt not eat of it: for in the day that thou eatest thereof thou shalt surely die" (Gen. 2:16–17).

First, the Lord was instructive; He began with a statement of what Adam could do: "Of every tree of the garden thou mayest freely eat."

Second, He told Adam what was expected of him: "But of the tree of knowledge of good and evil, thou shalt not eat of it."

Third, He clearly stated the *earned* consequences: "For in the day that thou eatest thereof thou shalt surely die." I emphasize "earned" consequences because it was a consequence Adam would bring upon himself by the choice he made. The Lord did not say, "In the day thou eatest thereof, I will kill you." That would be an imposed, forced consequence, and God does not do that sort of thing with or to His children. Nor should we. He forbids, but He permits. Children must be taught early that God does not punish people; people punish themselves by how they choose to behave. What we see as "punishment" is often, from a godly perspective, the self-imposed, natural consequence of the choices we make. It is a shame that we have come to cast God in the role of a fearsome, vindictive tyrant who is just waiting to get His hands on us so He can beat some sense into our heads and get even with us for all our stupid mistakes and ugly sins. It's this image of God that keeps many people away from religious commitments and activities, especially our youth. A moment in the life of Billy Graham's son, Franklin, nicely illustrates that: "I had this picture of this God in heaven who had, like a big stick, and if I surrendered my life, he'd just wait for me to go to the left or right and clobber me" (Van Biema, 69).

Mom and Dad, does that give you some hint about how to parent? Do your children make good choices and behave well because when they do, you lovingly and kindly show your appreciation? Or do they grudgingly do what they are supposed to do because they don't want to get "clobbered"? Think about that.

In the encounter between the Lord and Adam we find a parenting model for all parents to follow:

    1. Parents must first teach children what they can do.

    2. Parents state their expectations of their children.

    3. Parents clearly state the consequences that can/will be "earned."

    4. Parents allow children to make choices.

    5. Parents let the consequences of these choices speak for themselves.

The following scenario illustrates how this could be done in a contemporary family setting. The language here supposes a young child, but the same principles hold in the case of an adolescent.

Dad:	"Son, I notice you really enjoy riding your bike. It's neat having a bike. I sure enjoyed mine when I was a boy. What do you like best about your bike?"
Note:	Start on a positive note and be brief. Stop after a few seconds and give the boy a chance to respond. For example, the 32 words I used above take 11 to 12 seconds to say. When you ask a question, be sure it invites a substantive response. Don't invite a yes or no response. If the boy says, "Gee Dad, I don't know," probe a little. Say something like, "Tell me one thing..." The chances are 97 out of 100 that after you have probed only two or three times, the boy will come forth with a substantive response, as follows.
Son:	"Well, I like it because I like to run around on my bike with my friend, Joe."
Dad:	"Yes. Good example. Biking around with your friends can be a lot of fun."
Note:	Once an acceptable response is forthcoming, reinforce the response with an enthusiastic acknowledgment and perhaps even a bit of embellishment: "Biking around with your friends can be a lot of fun." This gets the momentum of the conversation moving in the right direction.
Dad:	"Son, I have one concern. You sometimes leave your bike lying in the driveway, and before I can drive into the garage, I have to get out of the car and move it out of the way. And besides, leaving your bike in the driveway could be dangerous. How can that be dangerous?"
Note:	In expressing your concern, do two things: First, state your concern calmly with just a few words. No lectures! Second, make your concern his concern by inviting him to tell you what he has to gain or lose.
Son:	"I suppose my bike could get run over."
Dad:	"That's right, Son. And why would that be such a terrible thing?"
Note:	Help the child see what natural consequences could do to him. Don't dwell on your annoyance, inconveniences, or the possible damages to your car. A 10-year-old (or a 19-year-old, for that matter!) could care less about those

	things. But the loss of his bike! Now that means something.
Son:	"Well, I wouldn't have a bike to ride."
Dad:	"And what's so bad about that?"
Son:	"Gee, Dad. I wouldn't be able to go with my friends."
Note:	Probe these consequences just long enough for the boy to get the message. Don't you tell him the message. Let him tell you. He'll be a lot more impressed by what he tells you than by what you tell him. Remember: never tell a child something he already knows!
Dad:	"I can see your point. That would be terrible! And I would never want to see that happen to you, so here is what I expect you to do. When you get off your bike, put it someplace other than in the driveway. Where would be a good place to put it so that it would be out of the way and safe?"
Note:	Again, say only a few words and ask questions that put the boy in the role of problem solver—with you. This gets you both on the same side of the issue.

At this point, another very important issue must be addressed. As I have noted, children raised in the same home by the same parents can be so different. One child will be delightfully compliant while another will challenge everything a parent says. As you read this scenario, you might say to yourself, "If I asked my kid those loaded questions, he'd have a heyday with me. If I asked him why it was so important to put his bike away, he'd give me the royal runaround by saying something like, 'Well, Dad. If I didn't put my bike away, my conscience would tear me apart. I'd become a basket case of guilt and probably need to be admitted to a mental hospital where I'd spend the remainder of my life under intense psychiatric care.'"

If you have reason to believe that such an approach would evoke a similar response from a child, don't use it. Rather, say very simply but directly, "Son, rather than leave your bike in the driveway, put it someplace else. I wouldn't want to run over it by accident, and it's annoying to me to have to get out of my car to move it."

For some children, that's all you'd need to say. But for others, the remainder of this scenario might be highly instructive. Whichever approach you take, (1) keep it noncoercive, (2) acknowledge compliant behavior in some positive, pleasant way, and (3) reserve the mention of adverse consequences until it is absolutely necessary, as is illustrated toward the end of this scenario.

Son: "I could put it in the garage, over to the side."

Dad: "Good idea, Son. You're a good thinker. That would be a great place to put it. Any other place that is as good as that?"

Note: A positive response such as this is very reinforcing in itself, but it also gives you an opportunity to describe a behavior you want your son to develop; that is, "Good thinking." Tell the boy he is what you want him to be. Find something you can build on. This is an example of selective reinforcement of other appropriate behaviors (as discussed earlier), and you want to reinforce those behaviors that are like, are related to, or which approximate the behavior you want. In this instance, the boy thought of a good solution. Being a good thinker is a highly desirable behavior, so it would be wise to say, "You're a good thinker." This is an example of how you build self-esteem.

Asking a follow-up question is good for two reasons. First, it helps identify other options. This will increase the probability for success. Second, it provides another opportunity for the father to reinforce the son's behavior.

Son: "Well, I could put it on the lawn by the driveway."

Dad: "Great idea. You're really using your head, Son. What a guy!"

Note: "You're really using your head, Son" is simply another way of saying "You're a good thinker." When using selective reinforcement of other appropriate behavior, it's a good idea to vary the words that are used to describe the desired behavior.

Along with the declarative "What a guy," it would also be appropriate to use a physical reinforcer such as a pat on the shoulder or a light pat on the back. Pairing reinforcers is a powerful way to make a point.

The conversation could end at this point, or, if the parent felt it was necessary, he could continue with a statement of earned counsequences as follows:

Dad: "And Son, by putting your bike in these safe, out-of-the-way places, your bike will not get damaged and it will always be available to you. If, however, you get care-less and leave your bike in the driveway, you will deny yourself the privilege of using your bike for 24 hours. (This is called contingency management or "Grandma's Law." Having something desirable is earned by doing something less desirable first: bike riding privileges are contingent on proper bike care.) What will happen if you leave your bike in the driveway?"

Note: When the aversive consequence for noncompliance is stated, be sure you use only a few words and keep your voice low and calm, almost matter-of-fact.

Make sure that the denial of privileges is stated in such a way that the burden for that denial is placed squarely on the boy's shoulders: "you will deny yourself the privilege of using your bike for 24 hours." Don't say, "I'll take the bike away from you for 24 hours." The "bad guy" isn't you. The behavior is the "bad guy." Let the consequences do the talking, not you!

When stating the consequence, be sure the time variable is clear: "for 24 hours."

Son: "You won't let me use my bike for a whole day!?"

Dad: "Close. Listen carefully, Son. You will deny yourself the privilege of using your bike for 24 hours."

Note:	The child will almost always try to dump the responsibility back on the parent. Don't say, "No, no, Son. I'm not keeping the bike from you..." Simply restate the fact: "You will deny yourself..."
Dad:	"Now, Son, let's go outside. You can show me what you are going to do with your bike when you are not riding it."
Note:	This is role-playing and simulation. It's a powerful teaching tool, as well as a wonderful opportunity to reinforce more appropriate behavior. Typically in such a situation the child is so anxious to do it right that opportunities to reinforce "right" behavior (strengths) abound.
Dad:	(Once outside.) "Okay, Son, here's your bike. Ride it into the driveway, then show me where you are going to put it."
Son:	(Jumps on the bike, rides it out to the street, then up the driveway. Gets off the bike and parks it in an appropriate place.) "There, Dad. That's where it will be safe and out of the way."
Dad:	"Son, I couldn't have done it better myself!" (Give the boy a hug, a pat on the back.)

This entire encounter will take no more than ten minutes, which is as it should be. It is brief, specific, direct, calm, and positive. These are the keys.

In the example above everything went very smoothly. The boy never resisted or argued. But, as all parents know, it doesn't always go that way. In fact, it seldom goes that way. Here is what you do when problems arise. As you read through these examples, you will notice that the same principles apply to problem situations as apply to those that run smoothly.

Suppose that at the outset the boy becomes belligerent and doesn't want to talk about it. Here is how you might handle that.

Dad:	"Son, I have a concern. Sometimes you leave your bike lying in the driveway, and before I can drive into the garage, I have to move your bike out of the way. Besides that, leaving your bike in the driveway could be

dangerous. How could it be dangerous?"

Son: "This is dumb, Dad. I don't want to talk about it." Or he might say something like, "Dad, do we have to talk about this now? The guys are waiting for me. I gotta go—now!"

Dad: In a calm, controlled voice and without any facial expressions that suggest anger or annoyance (don't let your countenance fall) say: "Son, how could it be dangerous to leave your bike in the driveway?"

Note: This is called the broken record approach. You simply repeat your question. DO NOT acknowledge the distractors. Don't say, "Now you listen to me young man. You will talk about it whether you like it or not! Now you pay attention and do what I tell you to do!" or "Your friends can wait. This is more important than play. This is serious business. Do you want your bike to get smashed or something?"

Avoid these reactive responses. They are counterproductive; that is, they only make things worse by giving lots of attention to the very behaviors you don't want. The basic principle of behavior that applies here is that behavior is strengthened by the attention it receives. If you pay attention to things children do that you don't like, these are the behaviors that will tend to increase.

Son: "Dad! I'm not wasting my time on this junk!"

Dad: "I can see you are anxious to do other things, but this is important. Now, tell me why is it dangerous to leave your bike lying in the driveway?"

Note: It is important to show some empathy and understanding: "I can see you're anxious to do other things..." But don't back down or become reactive.

Son: "I'm not taking any more of this. I'm outta here!"

Dad: "If you leave now, Son, without talking about this, your bicycle will be locked up until we have had our conversation."

Note: If you think it will come to this, be prepared in advance to follow through. Have the lock ready. Don't have to go looking for one.

Son:	"Hey, you can't do that! That's my bike!"
Dad:	"As I said before, you can choose to talk about this now, or you can choose to lose the privilege of riding your bike until you will discuss it. Which do you choose to do?"
Note:	By no means should the father try to impose his will through direct, hands-on control. That kind of tough-guy stuff is coercive and can come to no good. The parameters for decision making have been set. The child can choose either option, and it's okay with the father. The boy can stay and talk, or he can leave, which will result in a loss of his bike privileges. The father is not the bad guy.

If the boy chooses to talk, despite a sullen demeanor, just proceed as illustrated above, not saying a word about the sullenness. If the boy chooses to relinquish his bike privileges, that's okay, too. In time, the odds are extremely great he will soon be willing to talk so he can regain his bike privileges. Initially, he might go off in a huff, saying something like, "Who cares. It's a crummy bike anyway. If you were as good a parent as Billy's dad I'd have a decent bike." Expect this kind of "noise." Since the boy is desperate and not yet fully civilized, he will likely resort to about anything to get his way or to defer blame. If nothing is said about this "noisy" behavior, it will soon be gone.

When the time comes, and it eventually will, that the boy can simply no longer tolerate the loss of his "wheels," proceed as illustrated in the first instance.

Another problem that might arise during the discussion when you explain the consequence ("You will deny yourself the privilege of riding your bike for 24 hours") might go like this:

Son:	"What! You mean you'll take my bike away for 24 hours? That's not fair! Billy leaves his bike in their driveway all the time, and no one says a thing. This isn't fair!"
Dad:	"Let me repeat so you'll be sure to understand: When you leave your bike in the driveway, you will deny yourself the privilege of having your bike for 24 hours. Tell me, Son, what privilege will you deny yourself if you leave your bike in the driveway?"

Note: The father didn't get drawn into an argument over what is fair. Never! I repeat, never get sucked into a discussion about what's fair. That's a black hole from which nothing enlightening or satisfactory ever escapes. Furthermore, the father didn't get sucked into a discussion about what goes on at Billy's house. He simply directed his questioning as before.

After doing this a maximum of three times, if the boy continues to protest and refuses to cooperate, then use the strategy just discussed: "The privilege of using the bike is yours when you are ready to discuss the matter." Then be prepared to lock up the bike, if that's what the child has earned.

Choices and Consequences

The Christian model of teaching children what we expect of them, identifying what the earned consequences are, then putting the matter in the child's hands is based on principles at the very core of good parenting.

When we teach our children what we expect of them and give them their agency to choose for themselves, we must be prepared to let the consequences of their behavior function as earned reinforcers or earned punishers. What that means, simply, is that if a child uses his agency to make good choices, he will enjoy positive, reinforcing consequences. If he chooses to study hard and earns an A on the exam, our response would be, "Good job. You made a good choice and it paid off. Super!" (Twelve words and four seconds. Keep it short and brief.)

If, on the other hand, the child uses his agency badly and earns an unpleasant, even punishing consequence, the parent should respect that and allow the consequence to deliver the message: he chooses to not study and failed the exam. The parent would say, simply, "I wish you well on the next exam." (Eight words and three seconds. That's plenty.) Neither accuse nor condemn (John 8:10–11).

The parent would not say, "Well, if only you'd have studied, this wouldn't have happened," and on and on. Never tell a child something he already knows. If you do, the child will very likely do just the opposite of what he knows you want him to do. He'll make sure he fails the next test just to show who's running the show. (This is another example of countercoercion, or getting even).

Nor would you make excuses for the child by saying something like, "Your teacher just isn't fair. That test was way too difficult. And besides, he's such a poor teacher, it's no wonder you failed." (As obvious as it is that a parent shouldn't do this sort of thing, I am forever amazed at how often it happens!)

Allowing children to learn the sometimes hard lessons resulting from the choices they make is virtually always in their best interest. If we interfere with that learning by artificially softening the consequences for their transgressions, we are doing them a terrible disservice. As obvious as this is, I see it happening all the time.

I was recently working with a set of parents whose son had broken into a car, stolen a cassette tape deck, and was apprehended by the police when he tried to sell it. To keep the boy's name off the police record, the father pulled every string he could. Happily, for the boy's sake, he was unsuccessful. But the father managed to interfere by paying the fine imposed by the court.

This is a terrible thing to do to a transgressor. Though the hand of comfort and reasonable help should always be there, it should not interfere with justice. Just as parents should not interfere with a child's exercise of his or her moral agency, they should not interfere with the lessons taught by earned consequences. As tough as it may be for a parent to stand aside and allow that to happen, it is how Christ would do it, it is how Christ has done it, and it is how Christ will continue to do it. Hence, it is how we should do it! It is the only way to learn how to make good, healthy choices.

Imagine the disservice parents do when they consistently intervene to shield children from the consequences of their actions—whether at home, in the community, or at school. The wisdom of letting an individual learn from his mistakes ought to be evident, yet I am always amazed by how many parents seem determined to try to sneak their children into heaven by depriving them of their right to choose for themselves. Perhaps such parents fear their children will not choose wisely and that their choices will reflect badly on the family—particularly on Mom and Dad.

When children's behavior becomes the measure of parenting success, the stage is set for an invasion of agency. To assure success, parents begin to—or try to—force their children into behaving well. How the children behave becomes more of a social matter than a spiritual, family matter. To the extent that becomes the case, the plan of the adversary becomes the parenting plan in that family, and disaster is sure to follow in the form of children not trusting their parents, being disappointed in them, and even disliking them. The worst disaster comes when children are alienated from their parents and family.

I have heard time and again the lament of young adults who became alienated as youth from their parents. Young people who had been the objects of abuse, criticism, sarcasm, threats, put-downs, and other coercive behaviors. Then later, when they became young parents, they had little or no desire to go home. Home for them had been an unsafe, dangerous place. A place to escape and avoid.

Many, many young mothers have come to me in despair, crying, "How can I feel better about visiting my parents? My children need to know and love their grandparents, but I hate to go home. And when I do, I can't wait to get away. I'm only there for a few minutes, and I'm already making excuses for why I need to leave. What can I do?"

I hear that plea so often, punctuated with, "I never had a life of my own. I was a good person. I felt I had to be a good person to make my parents and family look good." Certainly our behavior and that of our children should reflect a sensitivity to how it represents our family and its name. We should honor that name and bring credit to it. But trying to protect it by shoving our will down the throats of our children is not right and in the long run brings both pain and shame to the parents. How often I've heard parents—now grandparents—lament, "Our children rarely come home to visit, and when they do they seem anxious to leave. We see so little of our grandchildren, and it breaks our hearts." (That's a quote, by the way.) When I hear these sad laments, I think of a comment by Gandhi, "Those whom we keep down inevitably drag us down" (Fischer, 311).

Parenting that allows children to choose for themselves is not easy. I suspect the most gripping example of this is when God the Father allowed His innocent Son, Jesus Christ, to suffer in Gethsemane and on Calvary for sins He didn't commit, suffering He chose to take upon Himself in the service of others. Us! What anguish the Father must have endured when Christ cried out in excruciating pain, "Eli, Eli, lama sabachthani? that is to say, My God, my God, why hast thou forsaken me?" (Matt. 27:46).

The lesson for all parents, so beautifully exemplified by our Father in heaven, is poignantly taught in this touching Father and Son relationship. Christ knew full well the anguish associated with the choice He made to atone for the sins of humankind, and His Father respected it. Because of our heavenly Father's respect for His Son's decision, even given the excruciating consequences, all of humankind has been blessed. As a Father, God allowed this to happen for He knew it must be allowed.

Our Father in heaven's willingness to allow His children to choose for themselves should be our model for parenting, regardless of how tough it gets when children choose in ways that distress us. It is among the greatest blessings parents can give their children.

"Powerless" Children

Depriving children of the opportunity to make choices tends to render them "powerless," and the research on the effects of that are startling. Such effects are observed throughout the animal kingdom. Dr. Hal Markowitz of San Francisco State University, a noted authority on animal behavior, has reported such effects in animals as including lethargy; reduced immune system efficiency; maladaptive hunting and foraging skills; a selection against those behaviors that lead to success in the wild, leading to a weakening of the gene pool; an increase in random, purposeless behaviors; an increase in bizarre, destructive, violent behaviors; and isolate behavior. If the conditions leading to powerlessness remain in effect too long, the consequences are "virtually irreversible."

These same effects are observed when human beings, like caged animals, are rendered powerless by those who impose their will on them: they quit trying; they remain unemployed or are employed for only short periods of time in low-paying, dead-end jobs; they are frequently ill; they are repeatedly in trouble with the law, sometimes for very serious offenses; they become loners who gravitate to other loners (Walker, Colvin, and Ramsey, 5–6); and if their state of powerlessness goes on too long, the effects are "virtually irreversible." My observations suggest that about three to five percent of those who have been raised in coercive, punitive environments where their right to choose has been denied, or who have been shielded from the natural consequences of their inappropriate choices, never acquire the ability to function well as independent, contributing members of society. Of those who do become independent, contributing members of society, many bear scars for the rest of their lives: marital problems, parenting problems, health problems, and more.

Creating powerless children can result as easily from overprotectiveness and oversolicitousness as from coercion. Both interfere with children's exercise of their abilities and agency. Though often done unintentionally, parents can smother children's growth opportunities with misdirected kindness: feeding them to avoid the mess they might make while learning to eat; dressing them to assure that they look nice in well-coordinated clothing; speaking for them to avoid the discomfort of hearing them struggle to find the words they want to say.

Once they have been taught, allowing children the freedom to choose for themselves is risky business because sooner or later, to one degree or another, they will surely exercise the prerogative badly. If the consequences of that unwise use of choice are allowed to deliver the message, great lessons can be learned—lessons that can be learned no other way.

But when parents jump on a child with a verbal barrage of condemnation—"I tried to tell you! But no. You wouldn't listen to me. You had to do it your way. Now look at the mess you're in!"—coercion enters the scene like a rampaging flood, washing away any good that earned consequences could have delivered. In fact, it isn't unusual in such a circumstance for a child to say or think in return, "I wish I'd have behaved worse than I did!" (This is another example of countercoercion.)

How much better to respond to a child's poor choices by quietly and lovingly saying, (Christlike) "I'm sorry you chose to do that and because of it having denied yourself your telephone privileges for a week." Compare that with this: (Coercive) "How in the world could you have done such a foolish, stupid thing! Sometimes you behave like you don't have a brain in your head. And for that, I'm taking away your phone privileges for an entire week! Maybe that will be the call that finally wakes you up!" Consider carefully these two responses to a misbehaving child. Now ask yourself, "Why is the first more Christlike than the latter?" Read carefully John 8:3–11, with emphasis on verse 11.

Though inherently fraught with risk, allowing children to choose for themselves is not optional. It is absolutely necessary to their growth and ultimate well-being. I say it again, there is no such thing as risk-free parenting. Our Father in heaven is a perfect parent. He made no mistakes, and still, many of his children have strayed. We are imperfect parents. We make mistakes. And we, too, have children who stray. Parenting is an inherently risky business, made so in large measure by the choices our children make. Our heavenly Father gave us the freedom to choose and in so doing, became the model for our parenting.

Margaret Wheatly, in her compelling *Leadership and the New Science*, speaks about the dangers of too much control in the management of organizations. But what she says about control in organizations is every bit as relevant to the family, so much so, that in the following quote, I have substituted *organization* with the word *family* and the word *leader* with *parent*.

> Anytime we see systems in apparent chaos, our training urges us to interfere, to stabilize and shape things up. But if we can trust the workings of chaos, we will see that the dominant shape of our [family] can be maintained if we retain clarity about the purpose and direction of the [family]. If we succeed in maintaining focus, rather than hands-on control, we also create the flexibility and responsiveness that every [family] craves. What [parents] are called upon to do in a chaotic world is to shape their [families] through concepts. Simple guiding principles, guiding visions, strong values,

[family] beliefs—the few rules individuals can use to shape their own behavior. (33)

would agree with it.

. Dr. Richard Foxx, fessional literature, ıavior, a punisher is behavior will con- .).

ıighted notion that are punishing (that ɛr saying to me, "I , every day, and he f the behavior con- ıer; it's a reinforcer. doing to the child, ːd. That's a natural ; parents lamenting their childhood years in indifferent home environments have told me, "Getting a spanking was better than getting no attention at all, so I did things just to get a spanking."

Think about that one, parents.

Chapter Eight

OUT OF THE MOUTHS OF BABES

Many years ago, our youngest daughter left a note in our bedroom. It was written to me. She wrote:

> Dear Dad:
> I had all the dishes washed, dried, and put away. You didn't even notice. I wish you and Mom would pay more attention to the things we do correctly than the things we do wrong. You will see that the correct out-number the incorrect. I love you, but I am not perfect. I need more compliments than criticism.
> Love
> Julie

And I thought, "Out of the mouth of babes..." (Ps. 8:2; Matt. 21:16).

That was probably the most instructive moment of my life as a parent. From that day on, I began measuring my every word as a father.

The behavior of our children can be a powerful indicator of our parenting. Here are a few behaviors that can tell us a lot about how we are doing.

1. *What children say and how they say it.*

Children mirror their parents in so many ways. As noted earlier, "Children act like the parents who raised them." I am reminded of a popular cartoon strip in which the mother was listening to the things her preschool daughter was saying to her dolls. As she observed this, an older child asked, "What are you doing Mother?" The mother replied, "I'm listening to myself." And she was absolutely right. Children talk to their dolls, their pets, their siblings, their playmates, their school friends, and even themselves very much like their parents talk to them. Sons of verbally abusive fathers tend to be verbally abusive to their girlfriends, their siblings, and even their mothers. Daughters who complain a lot to and about their friends tend to have mothers who do the same to their children and friends. An estimated 60 percent of abused children grow up to be abusive parents. Too often parents say to me, "I am talking to my children exactly the way my parents talked to me."

Parents, listen carefully to the things your children say and how they say them. Beyond just listening, I suggest you make a record of what they say and how they say it. Keep a pad of paper and a pencil handy, and without anyone but you knowing it, record your children's verbal behavior, including a brief description of the setting. For example:

Date/Time	Description of the setting	What was said & by whom
11/2 8:45 P.M.	We were talking about the happenings of the day.	Sally seemed to gossip a lot about her friends and said a lot of negative things.
11/3 7:10 A.M.	As the children left for school, I said, "Have a good day."	Jason growled, "What's good about it!"
11/3 5:30 P.M.	We were fixing supper together.	Andrea was excited about a play she's in at school and how neat the members of the cast are.
11/3 7:05 P.M.	Michael was playing with the dog.	I was so pleased at how often he laughed and said, "You're a good dog."

Usually within a few days—a week at the most—trends will become apparent. You will begin to notice that verbal behavior is greatly influenced by the setting and that some settings will evoke behaviors much different than other settings. Parents find this to be a revealing experience. They become less inclined to use words like "always" and "never" to describe how their children talk to others. One parent said to me recently, "I was shocked to find that my son actually said more pleasant things to his brothers and sisters than mean and cutting things. I guess I have been hearing only what I was listening for." There is great truth to the idea of "selective hearing."

Parents are sometimes offended at the suggestion that they actually take data (such as a written record) on behaviors within the family. I can understand that such a suggestion might be unusual, but it is not unreasonable. Rarely do parents have an accurate, precise sense of how others in the family behave. One parent, for example, was aghast at what the record revealed and said in amazement, "Did I do that?"

We are often surprised at how we sound when our voices are recorded and how we look when photographed candidly. It is very much the same with our behavior. How we sound and how others in the family sound can be surprising when recorded candidly. A well-kept written record will reveal those surprises.

Tape recordings are also useful tools for measuring the verbal behavior of the home. At different times of the day over a week to ten days, while family members are together but unaware, switch on a tape recorder and let it record for half an hour or so; then make a written record of what was recorded. Of course, such recordings should be handled discreetly. They should never be made public, never used to embarrass or harass others, etc. In fact, once they are transcribed, the recording should be erased immediately.

Keeping records within the family is not at all unusual. We keep records of our earnings, savings, and spending. Some people count calories. I keep an ongoing weekly and cumulative record of my running. When we take a trip by car, we often keep a record of how many miles we travel and how many miles we get to a gallon of gasoline. We keep track of appointments and time spent at selected tasks. If a member of the family is ill, we keep a record of his/her temperature, pulse, blood pressure, and so on. Elaborate systems have been devised for keeping a record of medications taken, athletic performance, the weather, stock market performance, and the list goes on.

It is no less reasonable to keep records of our behavior as parents. Like any other record, they can be revealing and instructive, providing insight for building on strengths or for redirecting weaknesses. They can be used as a metric against which to measure the effects of what we do. If you are in a quandary about things done or said in your home, start doing some recording. You will likely learn lessons you could never learn any other way.

A parent with whom I have been working was concerned about her young son's language around the home: loud, critical, sometimes profane. Trying to convince the boy verbally that he sounded bad had done no good. One evening she discreetly tape recorded his outbursts. After the other children had gone to bed, and in the quiet of the boy's room, the parent played the tape to her son. In wide-eyed amazement he exclaimed, "No! That's not me. I didn't say that!" He was dumfounded at being confronted by himself, and it had a profound effect on his language thereafter.

If such a strategy is used, some cautions should be taken. First, the recording should be for instructional purposes, not to just "get even" with the child. The contents of the recording should be used to put together a plan for making things better. It should not simply be an example of how bad things are. Questions like "What can we do to help you?" and "How can you manage your anger better?" would give direction toward making things better. A solution-oriented approach should be taken.

Second, tape recordings should only be used if the parent(s) have good reason to believe that they would be accepted by the children as fair and reasonable. If there is a chance the child will be offended or made suspicious of the parent(s), I'd recommend not using them. To make tape recordings more acceptable, it would help to record the children in other settings when they are aware of being recorded, then having the tape played back to them. It also helps to record them when they are behaving appropriately. Being familiar with the process could help make it more acceptable in "therapeutic" settings.

Third, tape recordings of family interactions can be used with and for the entire family and not just targeted on one individual. Used this way, it is unlikely that any one member of the family will take offense.

Fourth, as it becomes evident that members of the family are working to improve their language and their interactions with others in the family, it is essential that those efforts be recognized in a positive, sincere way. Remember, behavior responds better to positive than to negative consequences.

2. The places children go.

A child's actions often say much more than words. Dr. Murray Sidman, in his study of the effects of coercion on human behavior, has taught us that there is much to be learned about human relationships by just observing where people take and place themselves relative to others. Coercive relationships—that is, relationships in which one tries to compel, force, or threaten another into compliance—prompt the one being coerced to avoid or escape the coercer (Sidman, 109). A classic example I often use to illustrate this important point occurred in an airport while I was waiting for a plane.

Sitting across from me in the boarding area was a young family. Seated between his parents was a child I estimated to be four or five years old. He was excited about getting on the plane and, as is typical of a boy that age in that setting, he was expressing his excitement with a lot of boyish physical and verbal behavior. At last he jumped up in his seat and in a loud, shrill voice that could be heard throughout the waiting area, said, "When do we go, Daddy? When do we go?" His father angrily looked down at the child, raised his hand in a menacing gesture, and said, "Sit down or I'm going to smack you one."

The little boy sat down immediately and very quietly, convincing the father, I am sure, that the way to get a child to settle down is to let him know who the boss is in no uncertain terms! But what the father did not "hear" was the message the boy delivered with his feet. The boy quietly and timidly slipped off the seat next to his father and took the empty seat on the other side of his mother. He went as far away from his father, but got as close to his mother, as he could get. What this little boy was "telling" his father was, "You are a coercer. You are not safe, and I want to be as far away from you as I can."

There is a powerful message here for parents of children of any age. It is this: Our children's feet can tell us a lot about what kind of parents we are. Do they take our children (and grandchildren) away from us, or do they take them to us? When our children come home from school, do they come running to us with hugs and kisses, eager to share the day's activities, or do they slip away with as little notice as possible to their rooms, to the TV, to anyplace other than where we are? Just watching where our children voluntarily take themselves is an example of what we call an unobtrusive measure of behavior. Such behaviors are unobtrusive because no one is trying to purposefully influence the behavior.

Several years ago, I was in the Chicago Museum of Natural History and noticed a person standing off to the side and out of the way with a clipboard and pencil making notes as people passed by. Curiosity got the better of me, and I asked him what he was measuring. He told me that from time to time the administration took data on visitor traffic patterns through the museum to see which exhibits were the most popular, by age of the visitor. He was doing nothing to influence where people went. It was completely unobtrusive.

He told me of other unobtrusive measures that I found to be fascinating, including smudge marks on display windows from the fingers and faces of little children: "The closer they get to the display, the more we figure they like it," he said. Wear on the floor coverings: "The more wear, the more popular the display." Contents of waste disposed in containers: "The more museum literature we find in the garbage cans, the less attractive it is to our visitors. It tells us what to quit printing. It can save a lot of money in both printing costs and waste disposal."

Great lessons can be learned from unobtrusive measures, whether they are observed in museums or homes. Unobtrusive measures of where children place themselves relative to others tell us a huge amount about who is safe to be around. Here are several questions parents should ask themselves about how safe they are to their children:

1. Do my children confide in me?
2. Do my children like to just visit with me, just shoot the breeze?
3. Do my children seek me out for advice?
4. Do my children spend their leisure time in my company? (If I am in the living room reading the paper, for example, will they stay in the living room also reading or just "hanging out?")
5. Do my children bring their friends to the house? When they do, do they introduce them to me? Do they visit with one another in my company?
6. Do my children run/come to me when I get home?
7. Do my children invite me to participate with them in the things they do (either as a participant or a spectator)?
8. Do my married children enjoy coming home to visit? Do they go out of their way to be sure we have lots of opportunities to be with our grandchildren?
9. Do my older children call home on a reasonably frequent basis to just talk?
10. When I greet or speak to my children, do they respond with grunts of acknowledgment, then hurry on, or are their answers substantive, and do they stop to visit, even if it's for just a moment?
11. Do my children give me hugs and kisses without being invited or prompted to? Do they spontaneously tell me they love me?
12. When I talk, do my children make and sustain eye-to-eye contact?
13. If I'm sitting alone on the couch, do my children sit down beside me, or on the same couch, without being asked?
14. Are my children comfortable seeking my help?
15. Do my children respond positively to requests from me for help?

These are but a few examples of the kinds of questions parents should ask themselves from time to time. The answers can provide unique insights into how safe our children consider us to be and can alert us to the need to remove barriers that might unnecessarily put distance between us and our children such as scoldings, scowls, criticisms, threats, and so on.

All questions need not be answered in the most ideal or positive way in all instances. Moods, pressures, and conditions at the moment could influence a response, one way or another, which would not be generally indicative of how safe a child regards a parent to be. For example, while visiting our sons and their families in California, my wife and I attended a piano recital of our 8- and 11-year-old granddaughters. The 11-year-old's father was about to wish his daughter well, but she was mingling with a group of other girls and didn't want that attention. With a subtle gesture of her hand, she let him know he was not to come near her. That was not an indication of how safe he was to be with. That night at home, when he was sitting on the couch, she came over, sat on his lap, and gave him a big hug. That's the indicator of how safe he really is to her.

A daughter brings a boy home and wants to make a good impression on a parent who is otherwise sour and indifferent toward his daughter. To put their best foot forward, both daughter and father are cheery, smiling, and amiable. These are called "short-term behaviors" and can create a false impression of how safe an environment really is to a child.

Questions of the kind I've listed are useful only to the extent that they represent long-term behavior; that is, the way things usually are. In research, we call these "measures of central tendency." They are measures of things that give the best, most accurate description of how things really are. That's why it is necessary to answer the questions listed above within the perspective of time, rather than on the basis of a single experience or a particular setting. When we limit our answers to a single experience or a particular setting, the tendency is to overstate the significance of it. This can create a false impression of reality.

For example, an otherwise happy child comes home from school having had a bad day. The parent cheerfully says, "Hi, glad you're home. Come tell me about your day." The child grunts, "Nothin' to talk about," and slips away to his room. If the parent is not careful and does not put this response into the larger perspective of what would typically describe a happy child, the parent could either overgeneralize the child's behavior at the moment or self-denigrate, either of which is unhealthy, as follows:

> Overgeneralization: "What's gotten into that child? It seems that he is just turning into a little grump!"
> Self-denigration: "Nice going, Mother! You sure messed that one up. Will you never learn? Well, it's like I've told myself a thousand times, 'You're a crummy mother and should never have had children.'"
> or
> "What am I doing wrong? I really am not able to communicate with these kids. There is no respect from them. We don't ever talk."

Without a measure of central tendency, these are the kinds of barriers we can throw up between us and our children; these are the kinds of responses that can trigger unhealthy ranges of allied responses. In moments of quandary and stress, we tend to state things in absolute terms like, "I am not able," "There is no respect," and "We don't ever talk." The moment has become forever. We must put things into long-term perspective. That is done by measuring behavior over time, then making the changes the data tell us to make. Then we keep measuring our behavior and that of our children so we can stay on track. The desired outcome is a parent who is safe to be around: one who avoids criticism; threats; forced compliance; screaming and hollering; arguing and badgering; name calling; a down-in-the-mouth, woe-is-me countenance; parental logic and reasoning; sermonizing and moralizing; endless questioning that never provides a single answer to aid problem solving; comparing to brothers and/or sisters—well, you get it: safe from anything that drives children away.

The mother of a 15-year-old son told me of an experience she had with him that "said" just how safe she was to be with. One night a ferocious storm moved in. Lightning lit up the sky. The boy, a photography buff, wanted to take some time-lapse photographs of the lightning. Though it was 1:30 A.M., he asked his mom to share the experience with him, which she wisely did after pulling herself out of a warm bed and sleepily making her way into the stormy backyard. Though she might have lost some sleep to the clapping thunder and the flashing lightning, she got a lot of son.

The parable of the prodigal son is instructive. From it we can conclude that though the son's behavior was loathsome, his father was nevertheless safe to be with. As reprehensively as the boy had behaved, as disgusting as he must have looked and smelled after feeding and keeping close company with pigs, he felt safe to "arise and go to [his] father" (Luke 15:18). "And he arose, and [went] to his father. [And when] his father saw him, [he] had compassion, and ran, and fell on his neck, and kissed him" (v. 20).

In shame, the son recoiled. "Father, I have sinned against heaven, and in thy sight, and am no more worthy to be called thy son" (v. 21). Here again, we learn just how safe his father was: "But the father said to his servants, Bring forth the best robe, and put it on him; and put a ring on his hand, and shoes on his feet: And bring hither the fatted calf...For this my son was dead, and is alive again; he was lost, and is found" (vv. 22–24). His father didn't scold or berate. He didn't sermonize or moralize. He didn't say something like, "You're not kidding when you say you've sinned and are no more worthy to be called my son. What kind of a son would do to a father what you've done to me? You're a disgrace!" He didn't ask useless questions: "How could you have done such a stupid thing?"

Despite the father's complete acceptance of his son, he did not allow mercy to rob justice. The boy had squandered his inheritance, and it was gone. The father didn't go to the other son and say, "Son, we have plenty. Let's split the estate three ways." No, he told the boy who stayed home, "Son, thou art ever with me, and all that I have is thine" (v. 31).

From this great parable can be learned many, many wonderful parenting lessons, one of which is to listen carefully to what our children's feet have to tell us. Recently, while tucked away quietly in my room writing, three of our grandchildren came to visit. They asked their mother, "Can we visit Grandpa?" Our daughter told them that I was in a quiet place working and didn't want to be disturbed. "But Mommy," they insisted, "we want to see Grandpa." Thankfully, she let them. Their little fingers rapping on the door were like angels' fingers strumming on the strings of a harp. As they came into my room smiling and hugging and explor-ing, I knew I was safe for them. It felt so wonderful.

The feet and the faces of the multitudes of adoring followers of Christ remind us of just how safe he was, just how wonderful it was to be with him:

> Matthew 8:1; 12:15; 13:2 "Great multitudes followed him."
> Mark 3:10 "They pressed upon him for to touch him."
> John 4:40 The Samaritans "besought him that he would tarry with them."

What a great parenting lesson is found in the safety of Christ's presence. "Listen" to what your children's voices, faces, and feet have to say about how safe you are as a parent and learn to be safe, as Jesus was safe.

Chapter Nine

Pray in Your Families Always

"My prayer is that you make your family something beautiful for God." — Mother Teresa

I recall the experience of a teenage boy who, upon returning home late from a night out with his girlfriend, was especially quiet as he made his way through the darkened house to his bedroom. As he passed his parents' bedroom, he noticed a light was on and the door was slightly ajar. He heard a voice and paused for a moment to listen. It was his father's voice. The boy's father and mother were on their knees at their bedside praying for their children. He heard his name mentioned, with an appeal to God that He would protect their son and see him home safely. It was an experience that had a lifetime effect on the boy, an experience that should be instructive to all parents.

The message is clear: parents should pray for their children. I suggest to parents that they follow the advice of the Psalmist who said, "As for me, I will call upon God; and the Lord shall save me.

Evening, and morning, and at noon, will I pray, and cry aloud: and he shall hear my voice" (Ps. 55:16–17). As the parents of 6 children, the grandparents of 19, and the great-grandparents of 3, Louise and I kneel daily in prayer, mindful of each child, praying that all will be well and happy. Recalling some difficult years with one of his children, Billy Graham wrote, "He knew we never stopped praying for him" (Graham, 708). And with what result? That son is now carrying on Billy Graham's ministry!

Prayerless Christlike parenting is an oxymoron. No one prayed more than Christ. The wisdom needed to be a successful parent within our declining moral environment is rarely available without the inspiration and prompting of the Lord. "You need more than your own wisdom in rearing [your children]. You need the help of the Lord. Pray for that help and follow the inspiration which you receive" (Hinckley, 98).

Christ, of course, was the perfect example of one who prayed. He admonished us to do the same (Matt. 6:5–13) and reminded us of the blessings of prayer (Matt. 7:7–8). Furthermore, as odd as it might seem, prayer has become the object of scientific inquiry, where research has found it to have a "stunning" and "remarkable" effect on people's lives (Dossey, 157). In a recent CNN newscast (October 13, 1997) entitled "Faith in Faith," Dr. Herbert Benson of the Harvard Medical School, reporting on his research on the relationship between prayer, faith, and healing, said, "It appears that we are almost wired at birth to God to believe" and that through prayer and belief, healing can and does occur.

In a Christian home, praying for our children is as much a parental responsibility as is feeding them, clothing them, educating them, watching out for their health and well-being, and nurturing them. Parenting without prayer is like trying to steer a ship without a rudder, driving a car without a steering wheel, or exploring a new territory without a compass. Prayer is a source of comfort, direction, and wisdom that is available nowhere else. Pray for your children continually. Never forget that! As noted by St. James, "The effectual fervent prayer of a righteous man availeth much" (James 5:16).

Effective parenting in these troubled times, perhaps more than ever before, requires the "wisdom of God..., even the hidden wisdom of God" (1 Cor. 2:7) to direct and consecrate our performance.

We are repeatedly reminded of this by our mentors and ministers. It is *so* basic to anything Christian:

Billy Graham: "People...have to commit themselves to prayer and service in order to keep love growing in their hearts" (Greer, 5).

Mother Teresa: "Love prayer. Feel often the need to pray, and take the trouble to pray. It is by praying often that you will pray better. Prayer enlarges the heart until it is capable of containing the gift that God makes of himself. Ask and seek: your heart will grow capable of receiving Him and holding onto Him" (Gorrec and Barbier, 7).

Richard J. Hauser: "In prayer, we set time aside to allow God's spirit to join our spirit and to raise our hearts to God" (Richard Hauser, Professor & Chair, Dept. of Theology, Creighton University).

There should be no question in the minds of Christian parents about their need to pray for their children. My counsel to parents is to kneel daily, morning and evening, in family prayer so that children will learn what family prayer is and will experience their parents' commitment to it. Additionally, I appeal to parents to kneel daily in private prayer to the Lord in behalf of their children, addressing with considerable detail the needs of each child and thanking the Lord for the precious gifts of life He has entrusted to them. Mother Teresa sent a powerful message to all the world when she said, "We must bring the presence of God into our families. And how do we do that? By praying."

As with anything we do in life, we learn by doing. By *our* doings, our children learn as well. Surely this is particularly so within our homes and families. I never cease to be amazed at the power and influence parental behavior has on the behavior of their children and the generations of children that follow. Parent-led prayer and modeling are no exception.

One of the jewels in the treasury of our family "fortune" is the precious memory of an experience involving family prayer. It was on a Sunday afternoon. We had my widowed mother over for dinner. As we bowed in prayer, I asked our oldest son to pronounce a blessing on the food and to express our collective thanks for our many blessings. He was a soft-spoken boy, and his prayer was barely audible. Knowing that my mother's hearing was failing, I was sure she hadn't heard a word he said. After his prayer, I said, "Thanks for that lovely prayer, Philip, but we could hardly hear you." Without hesitation, he quietly answered, "That's okay. I wasn't talking to you."

With the seeds of prayer planted early in our children's lives, then nourished by our example in the home, Louise and I feast on the fruits of the harvest that has followed. When we visit the homes of our children, they are talking to God. Their children are talking to God. There is no thrill upon this earth so great as to kneel in prayer with our children and grandchildren held closely at our side and to hear heartfelt appeals and tender appreciations ascending to God.

Our children and grandchildren aren't desperately driven to their knees by trauma. They are drawn to their knees by a desire to remain permanently attached to the security of their spiritual roots. They are safe there. Is it any wonder that's where they would want to be?

Though the objective, aloof attention of the scientist has begun to take an experimental look at the value of prayer, prayer will never be something that will reveal its every mystery to even the most rigorous scientific inquiry. Paul taught us an enduring lesson about this while instructing the Corinthians. He drew an important distinction between "the wisdom of men" (1 Cor. 2:5) and "the wisdom of God" (v. 7). Then he reminded us that "the things of God knoweth no man, but the Spirit of God" (v. 11) and that by the Spirit of God, His wisdom is "freely given to us" (v. 12). He notes, emphatically, that to the "natural man" this is "foolishness," but to the spiritually minded that wisdom is "discerned" (v. 14–16). My wife and I got a glimpse into this mystery sitting at our dinner table in a moment never to be forgotten.

Over the years, we have hosted in our home students from many parts of the world: Egypt, Japan, Ecuador, Micronesia, Columbia, Iran, China, and elsewhere. Peculiar among these many houseguests, most of whom were young, single students, was a distinguished professor from a prominent medical university in the heart of China. He was in America for a year receiving technical training that was not available in China. Though this was his first visit to America, he spoke English quite well, and we were able to communicate with very little trouble. We hit it off well from the moment he set foot in our house.

We felt that it would be important, early on, to acquaint him with our routine and to invite him to participate so far as he felt comfortable. It was not our intention to impose our tastes or our value system on him, but we felt he should at least know enough about them to decide for himself how to relate to them and whether to participate. We knew that his taste in food might be such that he'd prefer to prepare his own meals, but he was certainly invited to eat with us, and we could share our dishes with one another. He was pleased at this arrangement, and we all looked forward to enjoying what each had to offer.

We explained to him our belief that "man shall not live by bread alone" (Matt. 4:4; Luke 4:4) and that we knelt in family prayer at mealtimes. We assured him that if this made him uncomfortable, he was welcome to wait until after prayer to join us. To our surprise, he expressed eagerness to pray with us.

The days and weeks went by with only Louise and me offering the prayers. But we could see that a slight initial uneasiness was yielding to a warmth and a contemplation about prayer. One day, as we sat down to eat lunch, he asked, "Could I say the prayer?" As he prayed, haltingly and awkward at times as he searched for the words that would reveal what was in his heart, we found ourselves listening to a child's prayer. He wasn't routinely asking a blessing on the food; he wasn't talking to us; he was talking to God. Tears welled up in our eyes. As Louise and I held hands, we found our grip getting tighter and tighter.

It was a short prayer, and as our tear-filled eyes met, he asked, "Was that a proper prayer? Did I do it right?" We assured him that it was not only right, it was magnificent, and that perhaps for the first time in a long time, a *real* prayer had been spoken in our home. He was pleased, then told us something that made this experience even more special. He told us that before leaving

China to study at an American university, he was asked by his professional colleagues to see if he could find out how it was possible that intelligent, well-educated people could believe in God. At that defining moment in this good man's life, a life for so long benighted by the philosophies of man, he found the answer to that question. He told us simply, "Now I know!" The "wisdom of God" was spoken to him "in a mystery, even...hidden wisdom, which God ordained before the world unto our glory" (1 Cor. 2:7).

A few years later, we visited him in China and were guests in his home. There, he prayed for us. We correspond regularly. He is still praying. In a recent letter he shared this touching moment:

> I want to tell you a true story. A young girl aged 13 told me she couldn't sleep very well for almost one year. She was nervous about her study and health. She happened to come to my office and saw the picture of our Father in Heaven that you and Louise gave me, and I had kept very cautiously in my office. Each time I looked at it, I gained the power from our Father. She asked me to offer her the picture. Although it was very precious for me, I still offered it to the girl. I explained [to] her about my wonderful experience during my stay in the United States. I told her that Christians are the most wonderful people I have met in my life. Two weeks later she returned to my office and told me that she is quite well because she puts the picture on her heart and sleeps each night. She dreams Father rocking her and saying stories to her. Since then she prays for herself every night. It's true that our Father in Heaven protects her.

Prayer not only brings the presence of God into our families, it can bring the presence of God into *all* families, into families everywhere!

Janusz Korczak, a Polish Jew who ran an orphanage for Jewish children during the brutal Nazi occupation of Poland, helped to bring "peace and calm" to the doomed (Kulawiec, 248). Among his many "mechanisms" was prayer. In his book *Face to Face with God: Prayer for People Who Do Not Pray* is found this prayer, a good one for parents:

I don't bring you lengthy prayers, Oh, Lord. Nor do I utter a lot of sighs.... As a rule I whisper quietly; but my prayer I express with force. With a bold look I aim beyond the clouds. Straight as a ramrod—because it isn't for myself. Grant children good will; help them in their efforts; bless their labor. Lead them not down the easiest path, but rather down the most beautiful one. (64–65)

This is a short chapter. Somewhat reflective of my prayers: short and sweet. The Lord's Prayer is 66 words long and when said reverently takes about 30 seconds. But long or short, the long and short of it is, pray for your children, and for yourself as a parent in these difficult times. It will surely help. Parents often complain, "Kids don't come with instruction manuals." Yes they do, and the clear, simple instructions on prayer have been available for nearly 2,000 years. These instructions, found in the scriptures, are in virtually every Christian home. Some Christians even carry them around in their purses and briefcases. For those who travel, they are in the bedside drawer of nearly every hotel and motel room in America and many beyond.

These instructions are disarmingly simple, requiring no special skills or expensive equipment. The physical requirements are simpler still. Children manage them with ease: closing their eyes, bowing their head, folding their arms, bending their knees. It is all so simple. So very, very simple.

It is a skill that can be performed in an instant. With a single attempt, you are a champion, and the hosts of heaven are applauding, cheering you on.

Join your spirit with His, and be prepared for small miracles:

God no longer parts seas, stops the sun, or turns people into pillars of salt. Instead we have...smaller, more personal everyday miracles...God tapping us on the shoulder, whispering, or at times shouting: "I'm here! I'm with you!" (Halberstam & Leventhal, X1)

What greater comfort could parents possibly want?

Chapter Ten

BE YE DOERS AND NOT HEARERS ONLY

The apostle James understood the need to translate words into action when he said "be ye doers of the word, and not hearers only, deceiving your own selves" (James 1:22). This is a familiar message throughout the scriptures:

Matthew 7:21 "Not everyone that saith unto me, Lord, Lord, shall enter the kingdom of heaven; but he that doeth the will of my Father which is in heaven."

Luke 6:49 "But he that heareth, and doeth not, is like a man that without a foundation built an house upon the earth; against which the stream did beat vehemently, and immediately it fell; and the ruin of that house was great."

James 2:26 "For as the body without the spirit is dead, so faith without works is dead also."

1 John 3:18 "My little children, let us not love in word, neither in tongue; but in deed and in truth."

The message is clear. Simply knowing, even believing, guar-
antees nothing. As I've emphasized throughout this book, parenting is our first and most important responsibility. No exceptions!
To lose sight of tl   it-
izens. Yet all arou   ht
up by parents w   ss
material gains. Cl   its
seek the pleasure   il-
ity are being prize   li-
ty. In all of these   ot
effectively parent   \s
noted by Christ,   1e
flock shall be scat

This chapter   :h
parenting skills ca   —
ways that parents   se
methods is diffic   as
Naaman the leper

Naaman was "   it
man..., and honorable,...but he was a leper." His wife's Israelite
maid said to her mistress, "Would God my lord were with the
prophet...[Elisha] for he would recover him of his leprosy."

After much high-level negotiation, "Naaman came with his
horses and with his chariot, and stood at the door of the house of
Elisha.

"And Elisha sent a messenger unto him, saying, Go and wash
in Jordan seven times, and thy flesh shall come again to thee, and
thou shalt be clean."

"But Naaman was wroth:.... Are not [the]...rivers of Damascus,
better than all the waters of Israel? may I not wash in them, and
be clean? So he turned and went away in a rage."

Naaman surely understood what he was to do, but as long as
he resisted doing it, his leprosy only got worse. (It certainly didn't
cause Elisha any concern. It was no skin off his nose!)

His servants pled with him: "If the prophet had bid thee do
some great thing, wouldest thou not have done it?"

Faced with no alternative but to suffer horribly and die an out-
cast, Naaman went to Israel "and dipped himself seven times in

Jordan, according to the saying of the man of God: and his flesh came again like unto a little child, and he was clean" (2 Kgs 5:1–14).

There is a great parenting message in this timeless story. If parents will do even a few simple things according to Christ's counsel, and behavioral scientists of goodwill, remarkable and even seemingly miraculous improvements will occur in their families and in their relationships with their children. I don't use the word *miraculous* casually. Seldom does a week go by when I don't hear that word used by a parent or a schoolteacher to describe the effects in their families or classrooms of what I am promoting in this book.

As an advisor to families, I regularly have opportunities to help parents with perplexing child-rearing problems. Time and time again, parents excitedly report their successes to me: "It's a miracle!" I am gratified, of course, with such responses, but I remind parents that miracles are not my intention. Miracles are too hard to replicate. What I want parents to learn are some basic, easy-to-apply parenting skills with which they can "train up [their children] in the way [they] should go" (Prov. 22:6).

Here are four easy-to-apply methods by which parenting skills can be strengthened. They will have a familiar ring. Put them to work in your home as needed and be blessed. They are: (1) measure the "climate" in your home; (2) create a positive climate in your home; (3) keep the faith; and (4) enjoy your children.

1. Measure the "climate" in your home.

A basic principle of human behavior teaches us that past behavior is the best predictor of future behavior. What this means for us as parents is that with a few days of careful observation and recording, we can get a reasonably accurate account of how everyone in the family behaves, particularly towards one another. The form on the following page can help you craft a picture of these interactions.

Remember to record the positive as well as the negative interactions. As noted earlier, parents allow about 95 to 97 percent of all the positive things their children do to go unrecognized, yet parents are five to six times more likely to pay attention to children when they misbehave than when they behave well. We tend to be a problem-oriented people, and it shows in how we interact with one another.

After taking data for a few days, parents are amazed at what they find. First, they are amazed that there are typically many more good things happening than they would have ever imagined.

Second, they are surprised to find that children aren't "carrying on all day long with one rotten behavior after another" (to quote a parent I worked with). They realize that even when their children are behaving well, or aren't even at home, they (the parents) spend a lot of time thinking about all the misbehaviors of their children. Thinking about such things can be as distressing as actually experiencing them or being a part of them. Furthermore, thinking about misbehaving children gets one primed to respond negatively no matter how the children behave. It becomes a "trigger" behavior, and within minutes after the children are home, parents are interacting with them negatively.

Assessing the Quality of Interactions between Parents and Children

Description of the Interaction	+	-

Third, after taking data for a few days, parents are amazed at how much they contribute to their children's misbehavior. They are amazed to learn just how easily and how quickly they attend to the things their children do that "bug" them so. Parents are typically there in a flash when children act out. When they do this, they are giving huge amounts of their attention and time to mis-behavior. Since parental attention (positive or negative) is the most powerful consequence in shaping children's behavior, what parents find after a little careful study of their interactions with their children is that through their attention they are actually strengthening the very behaviors that annoy and concern them the most.

Fourth, parents learn that none of the negative, coercive things they are doing day in and day out to get their children to behave better result in desired long-term benefits. What they find is that things just keep right on going, very predictably, as bad or annoying as before. Hoping for things to get better, without doing something different—something more effective—recalls the defi-nition of a fool: "Someone who keeps doing what he has been doing, but expecting different results."

Take a few days, perhaps a week, and measure the quality of your home environment. You will learn things you would have never imagined. I'd like to have a dollar for every parent who has returned to me with their data and said, "I thought my children were the problem, but it's really me." Recalling Pogo's ageless line, "We have spotted the enemy, and it are us."

When our children were young, and sibling rivalry, griping, complaining, and noncompliance increased, I'd just take data for a few days. Sure enough, I'd find that right there in the middle of it all were Mom and Dad, scolding, giving advice, trying to make the world fair, scowling, frowning, and asking dumb questions like, "Why did you do that?" etc. Louise and I would look at the data, tune up our own behavior, and soon things were running smoothly again—or at least as smoothly as one could expect with six children.

If changes are in order in your family, they must begin with you, not your children. "You can't continue to do what you have been doing (even though you thought it was right) and expect to unproduce some behavior in your child, when your conduct was one of the things that produced it" (Packer, 106). Or as Christ asked, "And why beholdest thou the mote that is in thy [child's] eye, but considereth not the beam that is in thine own eye?" (Matt. 7:3).

2. Create a climate in your home in which positive interactions between you and your children are the rule and far out number negative interactions.

As emphasized earlier, we suggest that parents never have more than one negative interaction to every eight positive interactions. In time, since the results of this are so wonderful, the parents will rarely if ever have any negative interactions.

A negative interaction is any interaction that demeans a child or strengthens an inappropriate behavior. For example, criticism, sarcasm, threats, screaming, hitting, logic, pleading, and useless questions are examples of negative interactions. While in the grocery store I heard the mother of a misbehaving child scold him and angrily ask, "Do you want me to give you a spanking?" I thought, what a dumb question. How did the mother expect the child to answer: "Yes, Mother. That's exactly what I want you to do to me. A spanking is exactly what I need, and the quicker and harder the better!"

Be careful, too, with the use of logic and reason. In your wildest dreams, can you imagine a disagreeing son or daughter responding to your logical or reason-based appeals by saying, "Mother, you are so right! How could I have been so dense all these years? From this day forward, I will heed your every word; I will bask in the warm, revealing light of your maturity and wisdom." No! It never works. I suggest that parents rarely allow an hour to go by without having several positive interactions with their children and with each other. These interactions, in the form of a gentle touch, a kind word, a tender smile, a brief acknowledgment of a job well done, an appreciation for kindness shown to another, needn't take but a few seconds and require only a few words.

"You were so kind to your sister. Thanks." Eight words and three seconds.

"Thanks for helping with the dishes." Six words and two seconds.

"You seem to be enjoying that book a lot." Nine words and four seconds.

Recently I expressed appreciation to my wife for getting some laundry done that I needed as I was preparing to leave town for a few days. She replied, "I appreciate your noticing that invisible work." Parents should acknowledge the invisible things their children might do such as cleaning their room, washing their clothes, picking up their toys, or demonstrating kindness to a sibling, etc.

If parents acknowledged these sorts of things even a dozen times a day, it would take less than a minute, but the benefits would be immense. Such small and simple things can produce great gains. But more is better. Hart and Risley documented that in what I call low-risk families, parents "gave their children affirmative feedback every other minute, more than 30 times per hour" (126).

Several years ago while doing research in some public schools, I enjoyed the great experience of working with two wonderful women, both elementary school teachers. As I observed them in their homes and in their classrooms, I was forever impressed at how sweet, gentle, kind, and unflustered they always were. They smiled and laughed. They encouraged and acknowledged appropriate behavior. They were everything I could ever hope parents and teachers would be.

One afternoon I was in the home of one of the teachers doing some planning relative to the project we were working on. She had to go to another room to get some materials, and as she walked past the overstuffed chair in which her youngest daughter was curled up reading a book, she gently ran her fingers across the girl's shoulders. Her daughter looked up and smiled. She looked back, winked, and smiled.

Later I said, "I'll bet you have a great relationship with that girl." She replied, "Yes. She is a wonderful girl. I'm just very lucky." I hastened to note, "I suspect that luck has little or nothing to do with it."

Nearly every week our daughter Laura and her husband Allen invite Louise and me, and other family members, to their home for dinner and comradery. As Louise and I enter their home, we make it a point to have many positive interactions with those present within the first 15 minutes of being there: hugging, kissing, complimenting, playing, encouraging, holding, and so on. Intermittently throughout the evening, we keep the momentum of positive interactions going, and it makes a wonderful contribution to the family and to the sweet spirit of the evening. It helps make the environment safe and comfortable, motivating people to return week after week. When we have lots and lots of positive interactions we are safe, and our children and grandchildren want to be with us.

Laura recently asked my wife to tend their two boys, Jacob (4) and Matthew (2). Louise was busy sewing a dress for one of our granddaughters, and Matthew was napping. I decided to give Louise a hand, so I left the office for a couple of hours and took Jacob on a walk through a wooded area a short distance from home. Jacob loves creepy, crawly things, and that seemed like a good place to go exploring.

We just talked, held hands, observed, listened, and had a wonderful time together. I told Jacob how impressed I was at all the questions he had about the woods and the animals. I told him what a fine boy he was. I complimented him on his interest in things. We laughed together and had a great time.

As we drove home, Jacob looked up at me and said, "Grandpa, don't never die. I love you." I knew then for sure that Jacob saw me as a safe person to be with.

The key is for parents to establish the quality of the environment and refuse to allow the annoying, disruptive behavior of unhappy children to dictate the mood or course of their behavior. Their countenance must not fall. During a visit with our daughter Roxanne, her five-year old son, Brett, and his friend were playing in the snow. The friend came in the house crying, "Mrs. Mecham, Brett hit me." Close on his heels was Brett defending himself, "But he hit me first, Mom." (Sound familiar?)

Roxanne was nursing her newborn baby. Rather than becoming upset at this noisy intrusion, she said quietly, "Brett, we don't hit others." He complained again, "But Mommy, he hit me first." "I'm sorry, Brett, but we don't hit others." Brett looked at her, paused, and said, "Oh. Okay Mom," and off he and his little friend went to play again. A brief, noncoercive response was all it took.

This reminded me of a wonderful experience our oldest daughter, Karen, had with her first-grade class. One of her students was acting out. She quietly went to him at his seat, got down on eye level with the boy, and kindly said, "We don't do that in first grade." The boy shaped up immediately, and that was the end of the problem. Of course, later Karen acknowledged his appropriate behavior, and the boy behaved accordingly.

Parents and grandparents must be safe people for children and grandchildren to be with. We teach them we are safe by having lots and lots of positive interactions with them and by remaining calm in tense moments when emotions could flare. The following account of a grandmother's experience with a four-year-old grandson is instructional. The grandmother was tending her grandson while his mother was at the hospital delivering a baby. Soon the father called with the news, "It's a boy!"

The four-year-old flew into a rage. "No! It is not a boy. It's a girl," as he ran through the house slamming doors, screaming, and shouting, "It's a girl! It's a girl!" (Obviously, he wanted a sister!)

The grandmother remained calm, "Though what I really wanted to do was scream back at the kid. It was just awful. But I decided to put all that tantruming on extinction."

Soon the boy went to his bedroom where he continued to tantrum. About five minutes later, he came out of the bedroom and said to his grandmother, "Grandma, it isn't a boy. It's a girl." Grandmother, without trying to convince him otherwise, said simply, "Let's go to the hospital and see for ourselves."

Looking at his newborn baby brother lying in his nursery crib, the boy accepted his baby brother. The problem was over. The grandmother told me, "It was like a miracle. It was exactly as you said it would be. This stuff is so wonderful."

Pleasant, positive interactions between parents (and grandparents) and children always, in the long run, produce the best results. You can count on it!

3. Keep the faith.

This metaphor has great relevance to the message of this chapter. Old ways are tough to leave, and even tougher to leave behind forever. It is so easy to slip back into how it was before, even when we know better, even when we want to keep doing better.

Though they had been companions of Christ, ministered to by Him and witnesses of His heavenly powers, once gone, His disciples went a fishing; they returned to their nets. There is a lesson of caution here for parents.

As you set your sights on the quest of creating a safe, happy, positive, Christlike home environment, you will be tempted away by that "subtle serpent" (Gen. 3:1, 4–5). He doesn't want you to have a happy home. He doesn't want you to have a good relationship with your children. He wants you to fail. He is pleased at your failures. His angels rejoice at your failures while our Father in heaven most certainly weeps.

Any attempt on your part to parent as Christ would parent is going to be met with resistance. Count on it! The mother of several young children recently commented to me on how easy it is to "slip back to being negative, even when things around the house are so much better when we are positive." As I go about giving workshops on parenting, I am amazed at the number of parents who want "to be reminded again about what we should be doing." A genius has been defined as a person who does what he has been told to do after having been told 12 times to do it. We all need to be reminded from time to time to do as we know we should.

When changing one's approach to parenting from negative to positive, the greatest challenge parents face is that of staying on course by "keeping the faith." To help you resist the temptation to regress, I encourage you to put reminders around the house to prompt you to stay the course: a note on the bathroom/bedroom mirror, etc. One father fastened a small gold safety pin to the palm side of his wedding ring as a reminder to be good to his wife (Tate, 97). Anything to keep reminding you to always be a Christlike parent, spouse, or person.

I also suggest that you keep some positive, constructive coping statements handy for when you make mistakes—as you will surely do. Coping statements help keep us from kicking ourselves when we are down. They keep us solution-oriented rather than problem-oriented, and they keep us moving forward with hope. Following is a list of coping statements you might want to copy and tape to your bathroom/bedroom mirror for easy access in times of crisis brought on by a slip of the tongue, a lost temper, or a moment of impatience (Feindler & Eaton, 111):

COPING STATEMENTS

"Uh-oh, made a mistake. I've got to think ahead."

"Controlling my behavior is tough. I must practice more."

"This is new to me. Mistakes are to be expected."

"This stuff won't solve everything, but at least it'll help me keep calmer."

"I have to remember that I used to lose it! Now I'm much better controlled."

"It's okay to feel angry; I just have to concentrate on not letting it take over."

"Some situations are going to be harder than others."

In your attempt to keep the faith, it is important that you be consistent and predictable. Broad swings from negative to positive to negative to positive create what we call "case hardened" children who in time become resistant to parents' efforts to improve the climate in the home. As with Aesop's fable of the boy who cried wolf too often, children will not believe, will not hope, that anything better will ever last.

It is, however, never too late to start. When you do start, should your children wonder what's happening and say things like, "You're acting really weird, Mom" or "What's going on here? Have you been attending another one of those parenting classes?" don't get into a long, drawn-out discussion about why things are different. Just say, "I'm glad you've noticed a difference. I hope you like it" (11 words and 4 seconds), then smile, wink, and leave it at that!

4. Enjoy your children.

Dr. T. Berry Brazelton, affectionately referred to as "America's pediatrician," has a "wish" that is good advice for parents: "At age 16 or 17, when my patients have their last exam, I ask them what they remember as children. Many have said, 'My parents always worried. They never smiled.' For parenting to be joyless is tragic. My simple wish is that parents have fun with their children" (Brazelton, 125–26).

I wholeheartedly echo Dr. Brazelton's wish that we enjoy our children. Parents stream into my office with long faces and fallen countenances. Their tears of guilt and grief flow freely and easily. But when they leave, they are usually smiling, laughing, and walking tall with hope for a better tomorrow. They learn to enjoy their children; they learn to have fun with them; they learn a better way. Despite how our children look, smell, or act, we must let them know we love them and are glad to be their parents. (Remember the prodigal son!)

When faced with parental adversity, we must emulate Christ and endure it with dignity, our heads held high. This might be our greatest test. Think of Christ before His accusers, His persecutors. When brought before Pilate, He was resplendent, "insomuch that the governor marvelled greatly" (Matt. 27:14). We must all strive as parents to pattern our own behavior under stress after the Savior's marvelous example.

The mother of a teenage girl came to me completely overwhelmed at her daughter's behavior. As we sat together in my office and she told me of her concerns and fears, she was so intense that just listening to her exhausted me. I thought to myself, "Wow, if this is what her daughter has to endure day in and day out, no wonder she wants to be anywhere but home. I would, too!" My advice to parents is to relax, to ease up, to come up for air once in a while, then work as hard at enjoying your children as you do at worrying about them! It's under these circumstances that children want to be near us.

Some wise person observed: "There are better things than curfews to bring kids home and off the streets at night: a mother singing in the kitchen and a dad whistling around the house" (Braude, 136). Referring again to the Hart and Risley study, quality parent-child interactions were characterized by the following: "They just talked;" "They listened;" "They tried to be nice;" "They gave children choices;" and "They told children about things"; thus, "They passed their interactional style on to the next generation" (77).

Changing the way we have always done things is seldom easy. On a recent Sunday afternoon, I was visiting in my home with a distraught couple concerned over the behavior of their 17-year-old son. He was a "good boy" who was at serious odds with the family over an upcoming move to a city several hundred miles away. The boy had been born and raised in the town where the family lived. He was a good student, an outstanding athlete, and a very popular member of the community. The father had taken a position with another company that required the family to move, and the boy simply refused to go.

Sitting on my living room couch, the parents recalled in anguished tones the hostilities that had built up between them and the boy over this move. Though they had "tried everything," the situation had grown worse by the day. By the time of our visit, the boy was no longer speaking to his father and was staying away from family and home as much as possible. In fact, he had assured the family that even if he had to live in a tent, he was not moving away!

During our visit, it was altogether evident that the parents were trying their best to force wisdom, good sense, and logic onto their son, and he wasn't buying it. By now, they were at their wit's end. They were desperate about what could be done to reunite the family, to convince the boy to join them in the move. Joy had turned to despair.

I introduced my suggestions by rehearsing for them the consequence of coercion as a means of making someone behave. I pointed out that the more coercive the relationship with their son became, the more likely it was that he would want to escape, avoid, or countercoerce (i.e., get even). After only a few minutes of discussion, it became obvious to the parents that they had been trying to coerce the boy, and his response to that coercion was exactly what one would expect. He was avoiding the family. He wasn't talking to members of the family, particularly the father. He was staying away from home as much as possible. He was letting the family know that he could make it on his own, that he didn't need them after all. Though the parents understood what had happened and why, they were still in a quandary about what to do. And when I made my suggestion, it wasn't immediately well received.

I suggested to the parents that upon returning home, they sit down with the boy and proceed noncoercively. We role-played to demonstrate what to do and say. It went like this:

> Son, you are correct. We cannot make you move, nor do
> we have any intentions of making you move. It is clear to us

that you have things going for you here that are just too hard to walk away from. However, since we love you and are so concerned about your well-being, we just ask one thing of you. We want you to take a week or so and make arrangements for staying here so that we can be assured that you'll be well cared for. We know you have friends. You have told us that your coach will even open his home to you. Please explore your options and then in a couple of weeks let us know what those are. In the meantime, let's get back together as a family and be the friends we used to be. Let's enjoy each other again.

The parents, particularly the father, looked at me like I was crazy. He stared at the floor, shaking his head, and in soft tones said, "It won't work. It won't work."

I asked the father if he would follow a medical doctor's advice to treat his son's physical illness. The father looked up and said, "Certainly I would." I then said, "I am giving you a behavioral prescription, and I expect you to follow it. I have given you a considerable amount of my Sunday afternoon without charge, and I fully expect you to do what I tell you to do whether or not you think it will work. Furthermore, I am willing to wager a steak dinner that if you do what I advise you to do, your boy will make the move with you. If you do what I have advised you to do, and the boy doesn't make the move with you, I owe you a steak dinner." On that light note, the visit ended. We were smiling and laughing. Hope was again in the picture.

A few months later I received a letter updating me on how things were going. The following excerpt brought a smile to my face—and set my mouth watering:

> Things have improved so much for us since implementing your ideas. [Our son] is speaking to his father again and things look positive for the move. The tension has decreased 100 percent. We send our thanks, and you can plan on that steak dinner we owe you.

Thousands of words have fallen on the pages of this book in an attempt to convince its readers of the importance of being a good parent, a Christlike parent. I attest to the effectiveness and goodness of what I have written. But hope for success is virtually nonexistent in the absence of parenting behaviors which tell children, "I'm glad you're my child. I'm glad I'm your parent." As Paul assured the Corinthians, "the letter killeth, but the spirit giveth life" (2 Cor. 3:6).

To solve a problem you must act. Wanting to act, without action, is meaningless. Determination to act without action is meaningless. Attitude without action is meaningless. We are forever being told that "attitude is everything." On the wall of the conference room near my office is a colorful, graphic poster declaring "Attitude determines your altitude." Not so! *Action* determines altitude! True, it's better to have a good attitude than a bad one, but a bad attitude followed by good actions is a lot better than a good attitude followed by no action (Matt. 23:3). This advice from Ecclesiastes is timely: "When thou vowest a vow..., pay it...: pay that which thou hast vowed. Better is it that thou shouldest not vow, than that thou shouldest vow and not pay" (5:4–5).

The science of human behavior has taught us that variables such as will, want, desire, determination, resolve, attitude, and so on, are only "antecedents." They are only mental or emotional statements intended to move people to action. If people don't act upon these antecedents, then enjoy the success (that is, the reinforcers) for those actions, the antecedents are meaningless, and soon the will, want, desire, determination, resolve, and attitude wane and die. Willpower is good, but do-power is better. Lots better!

Millions of people across the face of the earth *want* to quit smoking, but since the act of smoking brings greater *immediate* pleasure (the reinforcer) than does the act of not smoking, they keep smoking. And so it is with any noxious habit that should be changed. It is not until we act upon the antecedent and then experience success from that action that we really come to *want* to act that way again. We learn to want to do better by first doing better, then enjoying the success of doing better (that's the reinforcer). I recall it again: Christ told the multitude on the Mount, "Not everyone that *saith* unto me, Lord, Lord, shall enter the kingdom of heaven; but he that *doeth* the will of my Father which is in heaven (Matt. 7:21; emphasis added). And so it is with parenting. Simply *talking* about good parenting or *wanting* to be a good parent is "as sounding brass, or a tinkling cymbal" (1 Cor. 13:1).

A young couple came to me in distress: "We *want* to be good parents. We don't want to parent like we were. We don't want to scream at our children and spank them. We want to be in control of ourselves because we know if we do, we will all be happier."

For months, I tried to help them translate their wants into action. "But it's so hard to do," they'd say. "We are always so tired; then the children get on our nerves and we lose it. We just can't help it! We just can't help it!" Tears stained their faces as they passionately rehearsed to me their desire to do better. Days turned into weeks. No change in their behavior. Weeks grew into months. Attitude grew into resolve and determination, neither of which produced any lasting action. After a few years they moved away, still screaming and spanking, but not wanting to.

On the other hand, the parents of an able 13-year-old boy came to me concerned about the boy's academic failure. As we discussed the boy's problem, it became clear to me that he was getting a lot more parental attention for failing in school than he was getting for succeeding in school. School success was expected of the boy, and in the eyes of the parents, he didn't deserve any reinforcement other than the intrinsic rewards derived from success. The parents were quite convinced that intrinsic motivation, produced by academic and scholastic success, was sufficient; nothing more needed to be said or done by the parents. On the other hand, when the boy failed his assignments or his classes, he was getting an immense amount of parental attention. It was no wonder the boy was failing. After all, it was school failure that brought the greatest amount of parental attention.

I counseled the parents to reverse their approach in giving attention. I suggested that when the boy was working on his assignments, reading a book, or doing anything that even approximated homework and studies, they should make certain to occasionally attend to that in some appropriate way. We discussed and role played several of those "appropriate ways." I further advised that if the boy got a failing grade on an assignment or on his report card that they respond with empathetic concern, minus unnecessary emotion. For example, I suggested that they say something like, "I'm sorry you got a failing grade. We are concerned about your performance in school, and we know you can do well. We wish you luck next time. If there is anything we can do to help, just let us know. We love you, and we are so happy you're our son."

This was definitely not what they expected to hear. They came to me looking for clever ideas that would get the boy studying and magic words that would cut through all of his indifference and enlighten his mind. Since I know full well that there is no such thing as "the magic word," and since I prefer to treat behavior with science rather than with simple intuition, I focused my attention on behavior.

Though their attitude about helping the boy was good, their actions had not been, and the boy was failing in school. On the other hand, their attitude toward my suggestion was definitely *not* good. Despite this less-than-favorable attitude, I was pleased at their willingness to *do* what I advised them. Their attitude about it meant next to nothing to me. I knew their attitude would change once they did what I told them to do and they began having success for doing it.

As the parents were leaving my home, I reiterated my expectations of them. The father wasn't smiling, though his wife was. I was happy at signs that her attitude was improving. That was good, though not essential for success.

A couple of months later the mother excitedly told me, "You'll be happy to know that our son ended the school year with straight As and an A- in algebra. Furthermore, things are so wonderful at home!"

Despite their earlier negative attitudes, bless their hearts, the parents acted and they had success. *Doing* what they were told to do produced the desired results. The reinforcing effects of this success taught them to want to keep doing that which had brought success, and ultimately everybody won. As I hung up the phone, my thoughts turned to the appeal of Paul to the Galatians: "And let us not be weary in well doing: for in due season we shall reap, if we faint not" (Gal. 6:9).

The lesson to be learned here is that murmuring and complaining about child rearing is not eased by simply wanting things to be better. Something has to be done before there is any hope of things ever getting better. The Lord has commanded us to multiply and replenish the earth. A tough assignment! But he has also prepared a way whereby we can do that effectively. He sent Christ, who "went about doing good," to model what must be done (Acts 10:38). He has shown us how, but the doing is up to us. This book can only help you know how to do that. The rest is up to you. But remember Paul's promise, "We shall reap, if we faint not."

Follow the example of Christ, "[Go] about *doing* good" (Acts 10:38; emphasis added).

Chapter Eleven

What Manner of Person Ought Ye to Be

Christ's disciple Peter asked a compelling question: "What manner of persons ought ye to be[?]" (2 Pet. 3:11). In a way, Christ answered that question before it was even asked: "Be ye therefore perfect, even as your Father which is in heaven is perfect" (Matt. 5:48). How one becomes perfect, if that is even possible, is up for debate. But for Christians, one thing is sure: We need to be as Christlike, as perfect at following His example, as we possibly can.

For parents, this question and its answer are compelling. Suppose one of your children asked you, "What kind of a parent do you think you are? In answering that question, begin, 'I am...'" How would you answer? Here is some space in which to record your answer(s):

_____

_____

_____

_____

As for myself, I would feel safe in answering, "I am kind to my children and grandchildren. I am a loving husband, and I treat my wife with respect. I am absolutely true to my marriage vows which I took upon myself over 44 years ago. I am something of a jerk when it comes to timely remembering the birthdays and anniversaries of my children and grandchildren."

These are pretty typical responses—the sort of answers most of us might give. But I fear some of us—even some who aspire to be Christlike parents—would have to give different, less flattering answers. Consider the following:

I am too often found attending to things less important than my family.

I am easily upset and speak harshly to family members when things go wrong at home.

I am occasionally seen viewing filthy and degrading movies, videos, and/or literature.

I am inclined when angry or upset to use profanity and to even take the Lord's name in vain.

And the list goes on.

None of these are things Christ would do, yet many who are trying to be Christians do them all too often. And they continue doing them because they are so highly and immediately reinforced for doing them! When we behave in such ways, we are immediately under the temporarily pleasurable influence of Satan. The "subtle" serpent has beguiled us.

Furthermore, when we do these things, we know we are doing evil. The Archbishop of Capetown, South Africa, and Nobel Peace Prize laureate Bishop Desmond Tutu has reminded us that "evil is real. Many people think it is a figment of our imagination. And evil does want to spoil the good things that God wants to see happen. In many ways we are involuntary collaborators with evil" (24A).

The Media

Let's look at one example of how too many of us become involuntary—or even eager, voluntary—collaborators with evil that can affect our families. I have seen marriages destroyed and families shattered because husbands and fathers were caught up in the whirling cesspool of filth flowing out of the sewers of the entertainment industry. I can just see Satan with his angels, laughing and rejoicing. (A refreshing exception to this sad circumstance is the TV show *Touched by an Angel*, the message of which is "God loves you." Thank the Lord for the few people of honor in the entertainment industry who care about the well-being of society!)

One author put it well when he wrote: "In trying to give the Devil his due, too many artists trifle with the true nature of Evil.... [T]he proliferation of mass communication...has increasingly numbed us to horror, pelting us on a daily basis with stories of shocking brutality.... Given this climate, it's hardly surprising that Satan should have metamorphosed from a pitchfork-wielding fiend into the Armani-clad guy next door. Evil isn't only banal these days; it's local.

"For that matter, we no longer like to call the Devil the Devil. Instead of words like 'evil' and 'sin,' we prefer to talk about 'dysfunction' and 'anti-social behavior,' 'aggressive impulses' and 'mitigating circumstances.' [T]hese days, movies and television have made wickedness downright heroic" (Kakutani, 37-8).

But the fact of the matter is, wickedness is wickedness, not heroism. When we purchase a ticket to a movie, rent a video, purchase a magazine, or allow into our homes television programs that, regardless of how entertaining or high-sounding the story line might seem, trivialize sex, glorify and exploit violence, and/or profane Deity, we are voluntarily collaborating with evil (Myers, 497). And when we support the sponsors of these programs through the purchase of their products and services, we are supporting a social environment that is destroying our children. We are sharpening the swords of our enemies, and we are polishing their armor.

Maya Angelou, reflecting upon her remarkable life in her marvelous book *Wouldn't Take Nothing for My Journey Now*, hit the nail squarely on the head. Read her wisdom carefully:

> Some entertainers have tried to make art of their coarseness, but in their public crudeness they have merely revealed

their own vast senses of personal inferiority. When they heap mud upon themselves and allow their tongues to wag with vulgarity, they expose their belief that they are not worth loving and are in fact unlovable. When we as audience indulge them in that profanity, we are not unlike Romans at a colosseum battle between unarmed Christians and raging lions. We not only participate in the humiliation of the entertainers, but are brought low by sharing in the obscenity.

We need to have the courage to say...vulgarity is not amusing, insolent children and submissive parents are not the characters we want to admire and emulate. Flippancy and sarcasm are not the only ways in which conversation can be conducted.

If the emperor is standing in my living room stripped to the buff, nothing should prevent me from saying that since he has no clothes on, he is not ready for public congress.

At any rate, not lounging on my sofa and munching on my trail mix. (43–44)

As parents, we have simply got to come to grips with this reality and do better. We've got to *be* better, more Christlike, for our children's sake and for our own. Paul cautioned the Thessalonians to "abstain from all appearance of evil" (1 Thes. 5:22). Applying that caution to parents today would mean that we would not go to a movie that had even the appearance of evil. We would not allow a television program into our homes that had even the appearance of evil. We would not purchase literature that had even the appearance of evil. Can you imagine Christ watching filthy movies and bringing trashy entertainment into the house?

If you want to enjoy a great story line, stay home, turn off the television, and read an uplifting book (how about the Bible?), write a letter to a lonesome person, or do something wholesome with your family. One of our daughters and her husband implemented a TV management program in their home that discouraged excessive, unhealthy television viewing and encouraged reading and other healthy activities. They have been so successful that now, even when there is a TV program they want their children to see, the parents "nearly have to beg the children to do it!"

(Latham, *Positive Parenting*, 299–305).

Data on the disastrous effects of the media on the lives of children are mounting and are alarming. As noted by Walker, Colvin, and Ramsey, citing several studies on the matter, the increase in violence in school "results primarily from the breakdown of the family and the portrayal of violent acts in the media" (22, see also 38). We know that. It is a scientifically validated fact. Why do we keep asking the question "What happened at Columbine High School?" We already know the answer?

Citing a particularly foul movie aimed at youth in which adolescents are "defined through stylized evocation of shock and transgression," Henry A. Giroux concluded that "social conditions that youth face today, along with a callous indifference to their spiritual...needs suggest a qualitatively different attitude on the part of many adults toward American youth—one that indicates that the young have become our lowest national priority" (31–35). In a major review of research on "The Mass Media and Youth Aggressions," the authors concluded that "scholars in the field of mass media overwhelmingly support the assumption of a strong relation between televised violence and aggressive behavior" (Donnerstein, Slaby, & Eron, 228). It is easy to understand why Mother Teresa would say, "I see that Christ is needed in television studios" (*A Gift for God*, 5).

This is one of the great moral issues of our time, one that is complicating parenting beyond anything imaginable 20 or 30 years ago. Michael Medved, an outspoken critic of the entertainment industry's insatiable appetite for filth and the dirty rewards it generates, has correctly advised us as parents and consumers to "move beyond questions about what Hollywood makes and focus more on what America takes" (113). In the final analysis, the solution to this immense problem, where the cunning of the devil has never been more brilliantly displayed, will not be found in a repentant entertainment industry, a concerned government, the V-chip, or so-called "rating" systems. As one observer notes, "Many people wonder why governments that are clever enough to devise ways to shield children from the danger of prayer in classrooms should not be clever enough to shield them from the evils of vulgarity in entertainment" (Grimsley, 50).

In the final analysis, the solution to this burgeoning problem is found only at home. As Christlike parents, we must be extremely discriminating about what Hollywood makes that we take. There is no amount of justifying or rationalizing that will make evil into good. We must heed Isaiah's timeless warning, "Woe unto them that call evil good, and good evil; that put darkness for light, and light for darkness; that put bitter for sweet, and sweet for bitter" (Isa. 5:20). I've heard parents and children justify the viewing of unwholesome entertainment by saying, "It isn't that bad." Well, no amount of bad is good for anyone.

I think of that often when I think of the support given by "good people" to industries and enterprises which promote products and services that are counter to the teachings of Christ and dreadfully destructive to families and good parenting. So far as the entertainment industry is concerned, I am not advocating censorship. I am advocating Christlike behavior. I am advocating good sense. I am promoting good parenting within the framework of the Gospel of Jesus Christ. What the entertainment industry makes is its business. What we take is ours. Rising above such in the name of what is right is being in the world but not of it (John 17:14). It is remaining "unspotted from the world" (James 1:27). It is showing forth the "light" of "good works" (Matt. 5:14–16).

When I speak of this to concerned parents, I am often asked the question, "But what about my teenage children? I don't view those things, but they do. How can I stop them?" The answer to that question is *not* found in coercing them to stop. You may not be able to stop them. In fact, if you respect their exercise of moral agency, you shouldn't try to stop them by forcefully prohibiting them.

The answer to the question is found in teaching basic Christian values, modeling those values in the way we live, and allowing consequences to deliver their message. Certainly, parents must teach their children that to support such an industry (whether it be movies, videos, TV, live entertainment, or printed material) is wrong. It is evil. We must be forthright about that. "A society too squeamish to call evil by its right name has destroyed its first, best defense" (Gelernter, B1).

Next, parents must not support such an industry. That is part of abstaining "from all appearances of evil." And finally, to the extent to which they can do so without interfering with their older children's exercise of moral agency, parents should apply consequences which either remove the desire to engage in such behavior or decrease any future interest or involvement in such behavior.

Suppose, for example, that a child wants to go to a questionable movie and asks to use the family car. The parent's response would be, "You may use the family car but not to go to that sort of movie." The child protests, "Hey, wait a minute. You're interfering with my right to choose for myself. You're forcing your will on me. You have no right to force me to do what you want me to do!" The scenario would likely proceed very much like this:

Parent: "It might seem that way, so I can understand your complaint. Actually, we are both exercising our agency. You have your choice to go to that movie, and I have my choice to not support your going to that movie. Go, if you choose. That's your business. What the car is used for is mine."

Child "Dad! It's only a movie. What's the big deal?"

Parent: "I suppose it seems like only a movie to you. To me it's an attempt on the part of a vile industry to corrupt my children. I can't support that."

Child: "Dad, my friends have seen it, and they liked it. They're all good kids from good homes. They told me there is hardly any swearing or sex in the whole movie. And besides, it's a great story. You and Mom should see it."

Parent: "I'm sorry that they would endorse or support a movie that had any amount of sex or profanity in it."

Note: Avoid any discussion of shades of good or evil, or how much evil is tolerable in deference to some supposed degree of good. Stick with the value system!

Child: "Dad, you're just an old fogey. You have to get with it. You can't go through life with blinders on, you know. There's a real world out there. This movie is about life in today's real world, not the old world you grew up in. Get a life, Dad."

Parent: "It isn't hard for me to understand that my life does, indeed, span two worlds. I suspect you are absolutely correct in that. But there is an unchanging world with which I have chosen to cast my lot, and that is the world within which Christ wants His children to dwell, a world free of all evil. In a comparative sense, that certainly is a world different from the world today. I've made my decision, now you have to make yours. But it isn't easy. God bless you."

Child: "Does that mean I can't use the car?"

Parent: "No. It means you can use the car, but not to go to that sort of movie. How you get to that movie is entirely up to you."

The child might go off in a huff and might even find other means of transportation to the movie. But the lesson taught about what the parent believes will endure far beyond the child's anger of the moment and will help shape for good that child's value system as a parent.

A recent phone call from a concerned mother, combined with an experience of several years ago, serves as a dramatic example of WHY parents should stand their ground on important matters of morals and values and the long-term benefits that come from this.

A mother called almost in a panic. The call went like this:

Mother: "Dr. Latham, I'm beside myself. I don't know what to do. I hope you can help me."

Me: "What's the problem?"

Mother: "My 15-year-old son asked me this morning if he could have a video party at the house tonight. When I asked about the video, I found it was R-rated, so I told him he could have this video party, but not with an R-rated video. We argued about it, and as he angrily left for school he let me know that if I didn't let him have the party at our house, they'd have it at Ted's house, his friend a few doors down the street. I called Ted's mother—she's a friend of mine—and asked her about it. She said it was OK with her, that she'd rather have the kids at home watching that stuff than at a drive-in movie. What about that? Is Ted's mother right? Am I driving my child away?"

Me: "Your original position on the matter is the better one. Your son might be angry with you, but more than that, your son will learn that you have values and are willing to stand firm for them. Sure he might, in fact probably will, go to Ted's house, but all the while, he is going to be reminding himself that what he is seeing and hearing is not allowed in his house. In time, he will come to understand and appreciate that his parents have values that are worth protecting, even if doing so seems at the moment to be unpopular. And in time, when he establishes his own home, when he becomes a man and puts away childish things (1 Cor. 13:11), it will be your values that will be in place in that home."

I reminded that concerned mother that Louise and I went through the same "furnace of affliction," but we stood by our values. And now that our six children have "put away childish things," guess what values are nurtured and protected in the homes of those children. You got it! The values of the home they were raised in. No R-rated movies.

Mom and Dad, understand this, and understand it clearly. Make your home safe from the slings and arrows of the world. Only you can do that. It's your home.

Today's social environment is vastly different from the social environment of even a generation ago. In many ways, the environments of previous generations helped parents raise their children. The general social environment of this generation is a parent's worst nightmare. This is no time to equivocate on our values. The sooner our children learn what those values are, and the sooner they learn of our unyielding commitment to them, the better. The ears of others might be "dull of hearing, and their eyes they have closed" (Matt. 13:15), but you are wide awake and alert. It's good that kids know that. Children need to see their parents being resolute on such socially sensitive matters, as encouraged by Mother Teresa when she characterized the Christlike person as the one committed to "the Truth to be told...the Way to be Walked...the Light to be lit" (Noonan, 124).

The Lord's admonition to the children of Israel is so relevant to us today: "Neither shalt thou bring an abomination into thine house, lest thou be a cursed thing like it: but thou shalt utterly detest it, and thou shalt utterly abhor it; for it is a cursed thing" (Deut. 7:26).

Putting Parenting First

Some parents get defensive about their favorite abominations or even the solutions to family woes. Consider the following antidotes to family troubles:

> Work less and parent more.
> Play less and parent more.
> Consume less and parent more.
> Social climb less and parent more.
> Spend less time chasing fame and parent more.
> Spend less time in the pursuit of money and parent more.

Some people become uncomfortable—even angry—with talk of this sort about their troubled family, yet rant against the antidotes. The mere mention of these antidotes can offend them.

Christlike parenting is a matter of setting our priorities in order. If we seek first to be a Christlike parent, all else will fall into place. In his first letter to Timothy, Paul wrote, "if a man know not how to rule his own house, how shall he take care of the Church of God?" (1 Tim. 3:5). I find it interesting that the Lord puts family ahead of church. Shouldn't His priorities be our priorities?

Though Christian parents know they should put parenting first, too few are acting on that knowledge. Rather, there is a discomforting trend away from giving parenting first priority. The reason for that, as I have illustrated earlier, is easily explained in light of what we know about human behavior and what influences it. Scraping away all the distractors, protests, rationalizing, and specious arguments to the contrary, it boils down to this simple fact: If parents persist in doing things other than they should be doing, it's because doing those other things is more personally and immediately reinforcing than doing what they should be doing (Cheney, *Source and Control*, 73–86). Simply *knowing* we should place parenting first is no competition with other more pleasant and immediately reinforcing activities.

There are ever so many examples of what I mean. For some parents, remaining home with a bunch of screaming, crying, fighting children can be punishing, while being out of the home in a pleasant workplace with mature, friendly, supportive colleagues can be very reinforcing. Being at home with disruptive children and being confused and frustrated about what to do with them can be very aversive to a parent. But being on the job where one's skills bring immediate and personally rewarding results can be very gratifying.

Since we know that behavior moves in the direction of things that are pleasant and noncoercive, and away from things that are unpleasant and coercive, it is easy to explain why many parents prefer to work out of the home rather than in it, to be away from home rather than at home. Add to that the economic dimension which makes it possible to accumulate desirable material things that can enhance one's image socially, and the positive reinforcers for nonparenting behavior become so influential that logic, reason, knowledge, admonitions, even testimony to the contrary doesn't fare well in redirecting the behavior.

As I go about the country lecturing on parenting, I am frequently taken aside by anxious wives and mothers agonizing over their roles as the child raiser in their families. In nearly every instance, the woman loves and supports her husband, but she is anxious for the well-being of her children. I am convinced that absentee dads are a major parenting problem in families today. Most of these mothers would prefer less income and more of their husband's time.

Before parenting will be preferred over competing nonparenting activities, parenting must be more reinforcing. It is as simple as that! For that to happen, parents must create their own world, part of which includes learning the skills they need to be successful at parenting—the skills that make parenting the most reinforcing, pleasant thing they do. We know what those skills are, and we know parents can learn them.

A mother recently wrote me: "I can't tell you what a change these practices have made in our home. The principles work so well it's truly like magic. I am so amazed at how well it works! We're having a lot of fun with it.

"We have four young sons, and since using these methods, I have so much more energy and the peace in our home has increased ten-fold. This is truly a Christlike way of parenting. It's certainly not easy to change habits of ten years, but the results make the motivation great.

"I must add that it sure helps that my husband [and I] can work together as a team."

With effective tools and skills, parenting can become the most enjoyable and reinforcing of all enterprises. And how does anyone learn to do something skillfully? By practice. Lots and lots of appropriate practice. If we wait until a crisis arises and then wonder "What do I do now?" we are dead in the water. We have to predict what might happen and prepare in advance for such crises. We need to have thought out in advance exactly what we will say, how we will position ourselves, and what we should do when a crisis arises. We then have to practice what we have prepared.

A young mother was recently in my office. She told me how every morning she could hardly wait until it was time to drop her children off at the day care center, how she enjoyed her job so much because it got her away from her "screaming children all day." She dreaded weekends. She felt awful that she felt as she did, and she knew it was wrong. But knowing it was wrong was no match for the powerfully reinforcing effects of being away from screaming children and in the company of customers and fellow employees who were telling her what a great job she was doing at work.

But then she learned effective skills. Before long, weekends were no longer dreaded. She became more thrilled to pick up her children from day care than she was about dropping them off in the morning. She had to keep working because she was a single mother. But before long she became happier as a parent in the home than as an employee outside it. At last, she was happy and enjoying lots of reinforcement in both settings.

To the question, "What kind of a parent do you think you are?" I wish all parents could answer, "I am a happy parent because I have learned to create in my home an environment that brings my family and me more happiness and joy than can be found anywhere else." Then and only then will parenting take precedence over all other behaviors.

I see too many parents trying to make the best of what they consider to be a miserable responsibility they just can't wait to grow out of. My appeal to all parents is to become as Christlike as possible. When Christ instructed his disciples to be perfect, he was telling them to become Christlike. If our priorities and our behavior are in order, our parenting will become more effective and the influences of the world will be far less influential.

What is a Christlike parent to do? I suggest the following:

1. Earnestly strive to teach your children with love and patience.

2. Be a living lesson to your children of what you teach.

3. Create in your home a positive, happy, noncoercive, nonabusive environment that is under parental control and where the consequences for appropriate and inappropriate behavior are well understood by all and are consistently and lovingly applied.

4. Allow your children to exercise their moral agency; then let consequences deliver the message.

5. Keep your hand stretched out continually to your children.

6. Pray for your children continually, morning, midday, and evening.

7. Be continually learning and applying better, more effective parenting skills.

8. Remain above the misbehavior of your children. Be certain your Christlike countenance smiles upon them.

9. Keep Christlike parenting at the top of your list of priorities.

What manner of parent ought you to be? The parent you can be. Christlike.

REFERENCES

A Gift for God: Prayers and Meditation (1975). New York: Harper and Row.

Adato, A. (June 1997). Camera at work. *Life*, 96.

Angelou, M. (1993). *Wouldn't Take Nothing for My Journey Now*. New York: Random House, 43–44.

AP/Nicole Davis (1997, Sept. 7). Mother Teresa: A people's saint. Logan, UT: *The Herald Journal*, 7.

Baer, G. G. (1987). Children and moral responsibility. In A. Thomas & J. Grimes (Eds), *Children's Needs: Psychological Perspectives* (365–71). Washington, D.C.: The National Association of School Psychologists.

Bandura, A. & Walters, R. H. (1959). *Adolescent Aggression*. New York: Ronald Press.

———. (1963). *Social Learning and Personality Development*. New York: Holt Rinehart and Winston.

Benson, P. (February 1992). Religion, religious institutions, and the development of caring. Paper presented at the Lilly Endowment Conference on Youth and Caring, Key Biscayne, Florida.

———. (Winter 1997). Spirituality and the adolescent journey. *Reclaiming Children and Youth*, 5 (4), 206–09, 219.

Bernard, B. (Spring 1997). Drawing forth resilience in all our youth. *Reclaiming Children and Youth*, 6 (1), 29–32.

Biglen, A. (1995). Translating what we know about the context of antisocial behavior into lower prevalence of such behavior. *Journal of Applied Behavior Analysis*, 28 (4), 479–92.

Bijou, S. W. (1988). Behaviorism: History and educational implications. In T. Husen & T. N. Prostlethaite (Eds), *The International Encyclopedia of Education*. New York: Pergamon Press, 444–51.

———. (1993). *Behavior Analysis of Child Development*. Reno, NV: Context Press.

———. (August 27, 1997). Personal communication. University of Nevada, Reno.

Blum, N. (March 6, 1996). Yelling excites youngsters. St. George, UT: *The Spectrum*, A6.

Bradley, J. P., Daniels, L. F. & Jones, T. C., comp. (1969). *The International Dictionary of Thought*. Chicago: J. A. Ferguson Publishing Co., 553.

Braude, J. M. (1957). *Braude's Handbook of Stories for Toastmasters and Speakers*. Englewood Cliffs, NJ: Prentice-Hall, Inc.

Brazelton, T. B. (March, 1994). Early sitting. *Reader's Digest*, 125–26.

Brendtro, L. K. & Ness, A. E. (Summer, 1995). Fixing flaws or building strengths. *Journal of Emotional and Behavioral Problems*, Vol. 4 (2), 2–7.

Brendtro, L. K. & Long, J. N. (Winter, 1995). Rethinking respect. *Journal of Emotional and Behavioral Problems*, Vol. 4 (4), 2–4.

Brendtro, L. K. (Winter, 1997). Mending broken spirits of youth. *Reclaiming Children and Youth*, 5 (4), 197–202.

Briggs, D. (May 2, 1997). Graham looks back as American's preacher. St. George, UT: *The Spectrum*, B1.

———. (September 25, 1997). Seeking joy? Read the Good Book. Logan, UT: *The Herald Journal*.

Carlson, M. (June 23, 1997). Prom nightmare. *Time*, 149 (25), 42.

Carter, J. (1996). *Living Faith*. New York: Times Books.

Cautella, J. R. & Kearney, A. J. (1986). *The Covert Conditioning Handbook*. New York: Springer Publishing Company.

Cheney, C. (1991). The source and control of behavior. In W. Ishaq (Ed), *Human Behavior in Today's World*. New York: Praeger, 73–86.

———. (March 18, 1994). Aversive control: A call for research. The Sixth Annual Convention of the International Behaviorology Association, Guanajuata, Mexico.

Clark, R. C. (1971). *Einstein: The Life and Times*. New York: Avon Books.

Cobb, H. (1987). Children and religion. In A. Thomas & J. Grimes (Eds), *Children's Needs: Psychological Perspectives*. Washington, D.C.: The National Association of School Psychologists.

Coura, L. S. & Rocha, S. (Winter, 1996). From family violence to respect: Teaching parents to listen to their children. *Journal of Emotional and Behavioral Problems*, 4, 5–12.

Daniels, A. C. (1994). *Bringing Out the Best in People*. San Francisco: McGraw-Hill, Inc.

Donnerstein, E., Slaby, R. G. & Eron, L. D. (1994). The mass media and youth aggression. In L. D. Eron, J. H. Gentry & P. Schlegel (Eds), *Reason to Hope: A Psychosocial Perspective on Violence and Youth*. Washington, D.C.: American Psychological Association, 219–50.

Dossey, L. (March, 1996). Does prayer heal? *Reader's Digest*, 157–67.

Drummand, H. (undated). *The Greatest Thing in the World*. London: Collins.

Eftimiades, M., Goulding, C., Duignan-Cabrera, A. & Podesta, J. S. (June 23, 1997). Why are kids killing? *People*, 47 (24), 46–53.

Eye on America with Dan Rather (Oct. 30, 1997). New York: CBS News.

Feindler, E. & Eaton, R. (1986). *Cognitive-Behavioral Techniques*. New York: Pergamon Press.

Fischer, L. (1950). *The Life of Mahatma Gandhi*. New York: Harper and Row.

Fish, J. M. (Spring, 1995). Does problem behavior just happen? *Behavior and Social Issues*, Vol. 5 (1), 3–12. (Published by the Cambridge Center for Behavioral Studies, Cambridge, MA).

Foxx, R. M. (Fall, 1996). Translating the covenant: The behavior analyst as ambassador and translator. *The Behavior Analyst*, 19 (2), 147–61.

Frankl, V. E. (1984). *Man's Search for Meaning*. New York: Simon and Schuster.

Gelernter, D. (October 26, 1997). Surviving the unabomber. *The Sacramento Bee*, Forum, B1.

Gibran, K. (1958). *The Voice of the Master*.

Giroux, H. A. (1996). Hollywood, race, and the demoralization of youth: The "kids" are not "alright." *Educational Research*, 25 (2), 31–35.

Gorrec, G. & Barbier, J. (Eds) (1995). *The Love of Christ: Spiritual Counsels (Mother Teresa of Calcutta)*. San Francisco: Harper and Row.

Graham, B. (1997). *Just as I Am*. New York: Harper Collins.

Greer, C. (October 20, 1996). Our task is to do all we can—not just sit and wait. *Parade*, 4–6.

Grimsley, E. (April, 1996). In Points to Ponder, *Reader's Digest*, 50.

Guiley, R. E. (1989). *The Encyclopedia of Witches and Witchcraft*. New York: Facts on File, Inc.

Halberstam, Y. & Leventhal, J. (1997). *Small Miracles*. Holbrook, MA: Adams Media Corporation.

Hart, B. & Risley, T. R. (1995). *Meaningful Differences in the Everyday Experiences of Young American Children*. Baltimore: Paul H. Brooks Publishing Co.

Harris, W. (April/May 1990). Why most black men won't go to church. *Upscale*, 22–23.

Harsh words, crushed spirits (August 8, 1997). *Awake*, 3–4.

Hauser, R. J. (Summer, 1997). Praying with the spirit. *Windows*, 13 (4), 21–25.

Hinckley, G. B. (November, 1995). Stand strong against the wiles of the world. *Ensign*, 25 (11), 98–101.

Holler, A. (Spring, 1997). It had to get better. *Reclaiming Children and Youth*, 6 (1), 26–27.

How to train your conscience. (August 1, 1997). *Watchtower*, 118 (15), 4–6.

Hunter, H. W. (November, 1983). Parents' concern for children. *Ensign*, 13 (11), 63–65.

———. (April, 1995). Following the Master. *Ensign*, 25 (4), 21.

Johnson, D. W. & Johnson, R. T. (1995). *Reducing School Violence*. Alexandria, VA: Association for Supervision and Curriculum Development.

Jones, Jenkin Lloyd (Columnist). Quoted September 25, 1973, by G. B. Hinckley in his BYU Speech of the Year. Provo, UT: Brigham Young University.

Joselow, B. B. & Joselow, T. (1997). *When Divorce Hits Home: Keeping Yourself together When the Family Comes Apart*. New York: Avon.

Kulawiec, E. (Winter, 1997). A suitcase full of spirit: The last writings of Janusz Korczak. *Reclaiming Children and Youth*, 5 (4), 247–50.

Kakutani, M. (December 7, 1997). To hell with him. *The New York Times Magazine*, a special issue: God Decentralized, 36–38.

Keller, P. (1970). *A Shepherd Looks at Psalms 23*. Grand Rapids, MI: Zondervan Publishers.

Latham, G. I. (1994). *The Power of Positive Parenting*. Logan, UT: P & T ink.

———. (1996). The making of a stable family. In Cautella, J. R. & Ishaq, W. (Eds), *Contemporary Issues in Behavior Therapy: Improving the Human Condition*. New York: Plenum Press, 357–82.

Markowitz, H. (March 18, 1996). Behavior analysis and sociobiology: Strange bedfellows in the conservation of behavior. The Eighth Annual Convention of the International Behaviorology Association. Logan, UT.

Medved, M. (April, 1996). Our plague of pessimism. *Reader's Digest*, 112–14.

Merriam-Webster's Collegiate Dictionary (10th ed.). Springfield, MA: Merriam Webster.

Miller, B. (1998). Families Matter: A research synthesis of family influences on adolescent pregnancy. Washington, D.C.: National Campaign to Prevent Teen Pregnancy.

Mother Teresa. (December 25, 1996). *Detroit Free Press*, 4A.

Moyers, Bill. (January 8, 1995). There is so much we can do. *Parade*, 4–5.

Myers, D. L. (Winter, 1995). Eliminating the battering of women by men: Some considerations for behavior analysis. *Journal of Applied Behavior Analysis*, 28 (4), 493–507.

National Council of Catholic Bishops (1997). Always our children: A pastoral message to parents of homosexual children and suggestions for pastoral ministers.

Washington, D.C.: United States Catholic Conference, Inc.

Newman, B., Reinecke, D. R. & Kurtz, A. L. (Fall, 1996). Why be moral: Humanist and behavioral perspectives. *The Behavior Analyst*, 19 (2), 273–80.

Newsweek (September 22, 1997). Perspectives, 21.

Noonan, P. (December 1997). Woman of the world. *Reader's Digest*, 122–24.

Packer, B. K. (December 1970). Families and fences. *Improvement Era*, 73 (12), 106–09.

——. (May, 1992). Our moral environment. *Ensign*, 22 (5), 66–68.

Peale, N. V. (July, 1998). Have a sense of humor. *Personal Excellence*, 3 (7).

Peterson, J. L., Kohrt, P. E., Shadoin, L. M. & Authier, K. J. (Winter 1996). Building relationships with high-risk families. *Journal of Emotional and Behavioral Problems*, 4 (4), 13–17.

Ponds, K. T. (Winter, 1997). Shepherding spiritually adrift youth. *Reclaiming Children and Youth*, 5 (4), 216–19.

Reed, C. (1996). Eliminating whining in a 6-year-old girl. In Cautella, J. R. & Ishaq, W. (Eds), *Contemporary Issues in Behavior Therapy: Improving the Human Condition*. New York: Plenum Press, 367–68.

Reid, J. (June 16, 1995). Overview of violence prevention. Paper presented to the Workgroup on Improving the Quality of TA around the Topic of Violence Prevention, Academy for Educational Development, Washington, D.C.

Resnick, M. D., Bearman, P. S., Blum, R. W. Bauman, K. E., Harris, K. M., Jones, J., Tobor, J., Beuhring, T., Sieving, R. E., Shew, M., Ireland. M., Bearinger, L. H. & Udry, J. R. (September 10, 1997). Protecting adolescents from harm: Findings from the national longitudinal study of adolescent health. *JAMA*, 278 (10), 823–32.

Rhodes, W. A. (Spring, 1997). Discovering the threads of resilience. *Reclaiming Children and Youth*, 6 (1), 8–9, 25.

Rosemond, J. (March, 1996). Frantic family syndrome. *Better Homes and Gardens*, 52.

Rosten, L. (1968). *The Joys of Yiddish*. New York: Washington Square Press.

Schulman, M. (——). *Bringing Up a Moral Child*.

Seligman, M. (1985). Learned helplessness. In C. S. Hall & G. Lindzey (Eds), *Introduction to Theories of Personality*. New York: John Wiley & Sons, 551–53.

Sidman, M. (1989). *Coercion and Its Fallout*. Boston: Authors Cooperative, Inc., Publishers, 78.

Shriver, M. D. & Allen, K. D. (Spring, 1997). Defining child noncompliance: An examination of temporal parameters. *Journal of Applied Behavior Analysis*, 30 (1), 173–76.

Smith, L. (June 1, 1996). It's adults, not teens, at the root of society's problems. *Sacramento Bee*, 5.

Spink, K. (Ed) (1983). *Life in the Spirit: Reflections, Meditations, Prayers of Mother Teresa of Calcutta*. San Francisco: Harper and Row.

Tate, L. C. (1995). *Boyd K. Packer: A Watchman on the Tower*. Salt Lake City: Bookcraft.

Taylor, I. & O'Reilly, M. F. (Spring, 1997). Toward a functional analysis of private verbal self-regulation. *Journal of Applied Behavioral Analysis*, 30 (1), 43–58.

Teitelbaum, P. (March 12, 1995). Subcomponents of walking in parkinson patients and normal infants. Paper presented at the Seventh Annual Convention of

The International Behaviorology Association, Gainesville, FL.

Thomas, D. (April 4, 1996). Doing the Right Thing. Utah State University Arts and Lectures, and Partners in Business. Logan, Utah.

Tucker, J. A. & Tucker, P. (1983). *Glimpses of God's Love*. Washington, D.C.: Review and Herald Publishing Association.

Tutu, D. (October 1, 1994). An interview with Bishop Desmond Tutu. American Way.

USA Today. (October 15, 1997, p. 24A). World: S. Africa Apology.

Van Biema, D. (May 13, 1996). In the name of the Father. *Time*, 147 (2), 66–75.

Van Buren, A. (January 28, 1996). Daughter feels she can't do anything right in her parents' eyes. St. George, UT: *The Spectrum*, C2.

Vander Post, L. & Taylor, J. (1985). *Testament to the Bushman*. Harmondsworth, Middlesex, England: Penguin Books.

Wahler, R. & Dumas, J. E. (1986). A chip off the old block: Some interpersonal characteristics of coercive children across generations. In P. Strain, M. Guralnick, & H. M. Walker (Eds), *Children's Social Behavior: Development, Assessment, and Modification*. New York: Academic Press, 49–91.

Werner, E. & Smith, R. (1992). *Overcoming the Odds: High Risk Children from Birth to Adulthood*. Ithaca, NY: Cornell University Press.

Wheatley, M. (1992). *Leadership and the New Science*. San Francisco: Barrett-Koehler Publishers, Inc.

Winner, C. P. (September 17, 1997). In Algeria, "Unspeakable" horrors. *USA Today*, 11A.

INDEX

Abel, 8, 28
Abraham, 8
abuse, 41–42, 156; cycle of, 78–79, 162
action, 181–98; importance of, 31
Adam, 3, 145
adult children, 118–21
adversity, 20
agency, moral, 12, 101–02
Angelou Maya, 201–02
anger, 43, 77
angry boy at alternative high school, story about, 70–71
antisocial behavior, origins of, 77, 79–80
arguing, 73
attitude, importance of, 15–16
behavior, antisocial, 4; Christian, 62-63, 67; and consequences, 99; dealing with inappropriate, 66–67, 70, 77, 83, 124–25, 152, 188–89; forcing compliance, 156; in home, 9; imitating, 86; impact of parental, 51–52, 175, 185, 195; improving, 69, 116, 127, 140–41; lessons from, 106, 161–71; modifying, 17–18, 28, 31–35, 52, 67; motivations for, 55–45, 146; past indicates future, 183; recording, 163–64; shaped by positive reinforcement, 23, 55–56, 61, 106–07, 116, 117, 124–25, 142–43, 149, 165
"behavioral noise," ignoring, 18, 73,74–75, 90–91, 95, 103, 153
berating, 67, 69
Bible, 38–39; on reviling, 68
boy bumming around Europe, story about, 136–39
boy putting away bike, example of, 146–54
boy who didn't want to change shirt, story about, 52–53
boy who didn't want to move, story about, 192–94
boy with school trouble, story about, 196–97
Cain, 8, 28
calm, maintaining, 69–70, 73–75, 89–102, 112
character, forming of, 11
cheerfulness, importance of, 15–36, 20, 28, 35
child bearing, 3
child threatening violence, story about, 112
children, advantages of keeping at home, 85–89; allowing to make choices, 157; enjoying, 38–39, 191–92; expelling from home, risks of, 83–85; gifts of God, 25; helping to regulate media, 204–05; learning independence, 121; mirror parental behavior, 162; powerless, 157–58; relationships with parents, 44, 183; responsibilities of at home, 118–21; spending time with, 37–63; teaching, 38, 40, 41, 51–52, 54–55, 87, 116, 124, 129, 146, 154; teaching about bad behavior, 101–06; teaching consequences, 98–99; wayward, 7–9, 12–13, 15, 16, 50, 84–85, 93–98, 113, 115, 116, 117, who decide to leave home, 98–102; who threaten violence, 111–13
children's actions, learning from, 166–71
children's speech, log of, 162–65
Chinese visitor, story about, 176–78
choice, freedom of, 12, 205, 211
choices, 145, 160; responding to child's, 154–55
Christlike parenting, defined, 3, 11, 83, 208, 211
church services, participation in, 22–23, 61–63
coercion, 43, 45, 48, 55, 57, 60, 70, 76, 93, 124–25, 131, 159, 185; consequences of, 48, 56–57, 193
compassion, 73, 79, 83; shouldn't protect from consequences, 107–08
compliance, 6–62, 87, 169; and coercion, 101, 130; vs. values, 17, 19–20, 143
compliant behavior, acknowledging, 12, 52, 55
compliments, 141–42
condemnation, negative effects of, 158
conflicts, resolving, 75
conforming, 17
consequences, 12, 52, 55, 95, 104–10, 111–12, 115–16, 128, 145, 160; earned, 92–93, 104–10, 145–60
consistency, 191
coping statements, 190–91
countenance, 16, 26, 28, 35, 76, 116, 118, 137, 191–92, 211; and behavior, 25–28; Christlike, 25–26, 28, 116
countercoercion, 48, 52, 62, 130, 155, 158, 193

About the Author

Glenn I. Latham is professor emeritus of education and a behavior analyst. His professional interests are in child and adolescent behavior, with emphasis on improving behavior in the home and classroom through parent and teacher training. He has been a teacher and consultant and has written and published on a broad range of topics related to schools and families. He and his wife, Louise, have six children.